P9-ASB-128

TAKE YOUR BUSINESS TO THE NEXT LEVEL

A 90 Day Plan for Achieving a Breakthrough

Duncan MacPherson & David Miller
Co-Founders of Pareto Systems

OTTAWA, CANADA

This text is printed on acid-free paper.

Copyright © 2006 by Duncan MacPherson and David Miller

All rights reserved.

This publication is designed to provide accurate and authoritative information regarding the subject matter covered. Every effort has been made to ensure the accuracy and completeness of information contained in this book. Any slights of people, places or organizations are wholly unintentional.

Requests for permission to reproduce or translate should be addressed to Pareto Systems, 109-140 Commercial Drive, Kelowna, British Columbia, Canada V1X 7X6.

MacPherson, Duncan and Miller, David
    Take Your Business to the Next Level: A 90 Day Plan for Achieving a
    Breakthrough
    ISBN 0-9684401-5-0

Cover design by MEHco Inc. All rights reserved by Pareto Systems.

Printed in Canada.

Take Your Business to The Next Level

To Our Families

Acknowledgements

We have many people to thank for helping this book become a reality.

To our many clients over the years – both individual and corporate – we learned as much or more from you as you did from us.

To our head of consulting at Pareto Systems, Tom Frisby, thanks for your tireless contributions and unwavering loyalty. You and your team have helped take our business to the next level.

To our head of technology at 8020Platform, Darren Hennessey, thanks for your outstanding vision and execution and never ending commitment to continual refinement. Our clients run better businesses and lead better lives thanks to you and your team.

To Shannon Hull for being the quarterback of this project. Your impeccable professionalism in editing and your relentless project management skills were indispensable.

To our various mentors and to all the practice management and business development gurus we've worked with – especially Mr. Jim Rohn - thank you for your invaluable contributions. Our business acumen and our personal lives are richer because of your countless insights.

And finally, we would like to thank our wives and children. If ever the expression "Behind every successful man is a shocked and amazed woman" applied, it would be with us. And of course, we are both incredibly proud and grateful fathers of great kids. It's true, "You don't change diapers, they change you." Our kids changed us and we consider ourselves very fortunate indeed.

Table of Contents

CONTENTS

SECTION 4: REALITY CHECK *(WEEK 12)*

Pareto Systems Coaching and Consulting Services Spotlight
8020Platform Spotlight and Free Trial Offer

Introduction

After a successful multi-year strategic alliance between our two original firms, Duncan MacPherson & Associates and Mindset International, we decided to formally combine our strengths by establishing Pareto Systems in 2000.

We called our company Pareto Systems because of our fascination with the Pareto Principal, also known as the 80/20 rule. Our objective has always been to help entrepreneurs capitalize on the 80/20 rule and create a precise and efficient business in the process.

Because of our fixation on predictable execution and quantifiable results, our business development and practice management coaching and consulting services grew steadily. In 2003, we unveiled the Pareto Platform — now referred to as the 8020Platform — a one-of-a-kind business-building dashboard that integrates time-tested best-practices with a turnkey, web-based Client Relationship Management (CRM) system. Entrepreneurs from a variety of sectors in the marketplace use the Platform everyday to consistently manage and maximize their client relationships. We haven't looked back since.

It's funny how the word entrepreneur conjures up different meanings for different people. Some people think it's a French word for someone who works at home in their underwear (that would make for a strange Casual Friday if you think about it). Others think it describes someone who can't hold a real job or is a dreamer or serial opportunity chaser. In truth, an entrepreneur is someone who has a vision for how to bring value to clients and is persuasive, dedicated, motivated and resilient. Rather than simply have a job and make money, they want to build something that is worth a lot of money while maximizing their personal fulfilment.

As you are about to read, we are going to walk you through our process that will enable you to take your business to the next level. Like any book on this topic, there are countless ideas to be found in these pages. Unlike a lot of books on this topic, you can be rest assured that everything we suggest has been proven to work. Not a single concept is theoretical or on trial. Everything has been time-tested by ourselves in our own business and by the coaching and consulting clients who have hired us over the years.

But it doesn't stop there. Most authors tell you "why" you should be using their ideas and concepts. We won't leave you hanging like that. We'll also show you "how" to implement our ideas. The Actionable CD-ROM in the back of this book has a vast array of turnkey templates and concepts that you can translate into results. Because after all, you read a book to get better results, not just ideas, right?

At the risk of belabouring the point, a lot of people tell us that they like our ideas and creativity. We aren't creative. Any appearance of creativity stems from our ability to conceal our sources. Our sources are the business development masters we have studied and the feedback and results achieved by our clients over the years. So strive to implement the ideas you like, ASAP!

We say that because we believe the value of reading a book begins when you are finished reading it. If you can execute on the relevant concepts quickly and quantify the impact, well, then reading this book will have been a good investment. Just don't delay. Don't let the Law of Diminishing Intent rob you of the value of what's in here. You've heard the old saying, "After all is said and done, more is often said than done."

Our STAR Business Planning Process

Throughout this book, we are going to walk you through the exact process we use with our coaching and consulting clients as well as within our 8020Platform, framed by our business development acronym STAR. One of the objectives we hope you will achieve is that you will create a personalized business development plan using our methodology. With our coaching and consulting process as well as with our 8020Platform, we are constantly urging entrepreneurs to create and rely on a business development plan. This book has been written, along with the companion CD-ROM, to urge you to do the same.

The purpose of a plan is to enable you to stop for a second and kick your own tires and conduct a personalized, state-of-the-nation regarding your business. Our goal is that this book will force you to think things through and then crystallize your thoughts on paper to create a guidance system going forward. We use STAR because we feel it represents what we like to think of as the four cornerstones of a good, solid plan.

The *S* in STAR is the Strategic Analysis. Analyze your business. If you think about where you are today and where you want to be in the next 12 months, the space between those two places, between today and next year, is called *the gap*. So it is important to conduct a gap analysis. Analyze what needs to occur in your business to take you to that next level, to cross the gap.

Think of STAR as if it were a combination lock. Each of these letters represents a number in the combination. If you dial in all the numbers in the combination in the right sequence, good things happen.

The *T* stands for Targets and Goals. After the Strategic Analysis process, we proceed to goal-setting and the examination of targets – where you see yourself in the future.

The heavy work begins with the *A* in STAR. Actions! These are the activities you'll engage in to achieve your desired results. Based upon the Law of Cause and Effect, you'll identify the activities you should practice on an ongoing basis in order to meet the productivity goals you've set.

The *R* is the Reality Check. This simple process will hold you accountable as you embark on the journey.

As you go through this process, you may have one of the following three reactions:

1. I can't believe how much I'm doing wrong! This book has revealed some majors flaws in my approach.
2. I'm actually doing ok. This is a good validation.

3. I'm on the verge of a breakthrough and this is going to tip me over to a whole new level.

Either way, if you feel you need to make some dramatic adjustments, minor adjustments or simply stay the course you're on, we feel confident that the book will be of value to you. We must say that while there are numerous universal issues addressed in this book that affect virtually all entrepreneurs, our mindset and philosophy is especially effective for professionals in the knowledge-for-profit business who focus on long term client relationships. If you "think for a living" such as some of the professions listed below, well we can say with certainty that these concepts and processes will serve you well:

- Financial Advisor
- Accountant
- Lawyer
- Consultant
- Architect
- Engineer
- Contractor
- Wholesaler
- Medical Professional

That said, not everything in the format we present it in will be appropriate for all readers. Nor are we suggesting that this will address every issue and episode that matters in entrepreneurship. Far from it. Again, while we're confident that we'll trigger a few "Eureka Moments" as you read this, what we are really hoping you'll do is select the concepts that are appropriate to you and customize them to suit your own style and situation.

One last point. Do not be mislead by the apparent simplicity of some of the concepts we discuss. We live in an era where people are looking for a dramatic idea or a silver bullet. We have seen countless examples of downright basic concepts executed flawlessly that consequently generate staggering results.

For example, a while back we urged our clients to send Thanksgiving Cards to their clients rather than holiday cards in December. Our logic was simple, virtually everyone sends holiday cards in December and often it seems like the senders are just going through the motions. The Thanksgiving cards are unique and they stand out. Countless clients have made this minor adjustment and realized major improvements as a result.

And keep in mind, this book has been written in a sequential way that will enable you to build on your momentum. All 17 templates within the Actionable CD-ROM can be implemented within the next 12 weeks and, in the process, should take your business to the next level.

On behalf of everyone at Pareto Systems and at 8020Platform, we wish you great success as you embark on this journey. We'd love to hear from you, visit our website and drop us a line sometime.

Duncan and David

Section 1: Strategic Analysis

Your Untapped Opportunities and Overlooked Vulnerabilities

"Order is a temporary illusion. Strategy is a moving target."

– Rosebeth Moss Cantor

The first section of this book deals with investing your past into your future. We've all done a lot of things right over the years and we've all made a few mistakes here and there. Well, going forward the goal is to try not to repeat those errors in judgment while building on positive momentum. We'll define and refine the sources of our past momentum and make some minor adjustments. Those minor adjustments can lead to major improvements. There's a law in business called the Law of Optimization. (You'll soon realize we really like universal laws of business and life.) The Law of Optimization states that no matter how well an approach or process works it can always be refined and improved upon, even if those refinements and improvements are very subtle.

The second point deals with respecting the Reality Principle. Peter Drucker, legendary management authority and elder statesman of quality in business, simply said, "As an entrepreneur you have to deal with things as they are, not as you wish they were." We can relate. The vast majority of entrepreneurs we know are incredibly optimistic and even sometimes optimistic to a fault, where it actually affects judgment. We understand because we are also entrepreneurs and sometimes we don't always deal with today's realities. Instead, we sometimes subconsciously tend to focus on how good things will be in the future. The Reality Principle simply reminds us we can't always trust our own judgment or believe our own hype. To be objective we have to be brutally honest with ourselves and have a process that forces us out of our vacuum.

Identify Untapped Opportunities

In the spirit of striving to achieve clarity, one of the first things you want to do as part of Strategic Analysis is identify untapped opportunities in your business. Every entrepreneur we've ever met, to varying degrees, was sitting on a virtual gold mine of untapped opportunity. Most don't realize it. *Acres of Diamonds*, a great little book, by Russell Cromwell re-enforces this. If you haven't read it, it's a story about an ambitious farmer who got a little bored and wanted to go out in the world to find his pot of gold. He sold his farm to raise some money and away he went. He ended up being a pauper. Meanwhile, the farm he sold turned out to be loaded with diamonds. We see entrepreneurs – again, to varying degrees – sitting on those acres of unrealized wealth. One of the most tangibly rewarding aspects of the solutions we provide is helping business owners iden- tify their own untapped potential.

Remember

- Sound judgment leads to good decisions.
- Apply the Law of Optimization and the Reality Principle as you analyze your business.

Take Action Now! *(Week 1)*

- Open the STAR Business Planning tool in the Actionable CD-ROM to begin the process of gaining clarity for your own untapped opportunities and overlooked vulnerabilities.

The Loyalty Ladder

"It's more important to reach people who count than to count the number of people you are reaching."

– Marketing Maxim

In keeping with striving to identify your untapped opportunities, your next step is to establish what we refer to as your marketing pillars. When we sit down with an entrepreneur and scrutinize his or her business, one of the first things we'll do is draw 3 vertical lines on a sheet of paper. Each line is a pillar representing an existing or prospective target marketing opportunity. We call them pillars because, in a perfect world, you want a business built on a strong foundation that creates multiple income streams. These target markets, or pillars, are designed to create steady streams of predictable, sustainable business. Let's define each of the fundamental pillars that can be created for virtually any business. The first and most important pillar, and this should be self-evident, is made up of your **existing clients**. They are the most valuable asset you'll ever possess. Your client relationships are proprietary and often take years to nurture and maximize in terms of their potential. Too many entrepreneurs strive to pursue new clients yet leave existing clients twisting in the wind. As you'll see in a moment, this becomes a huge untapped opportunity.

The second pillar represents **promotional partners**. These are strategic alliances - the people in the marketplace with whom you collaborate. The third pillar represents your **prospective target markets** based on geographic, demographic and/or socio-economic opportunities available to you. Later in the book, we'll be expanding on your second and third pillars, but for now lets zero-in on your most important untapped opportunity – your existing client relationships. Obviously we don't know how many clients you have right now and frankly it doesn't really matter. What does matter, however, is your existing clients represent what we call your *inner circle*. And as we've said, your inner circle of clients is the most valuable asset you'll ever possess. A powerful and immutable marketing rule referred to as The Rule of 52 exemplifies this point. It states that every single client you have right now in your inner circle has their own personal inner circle of approximately 52 friends, family members and business associates. Some have more, some have less, but again that's not the point. Do the math. If you have, for example, 500 clients. What's 500 times 52? The answer? A lot. 500 times 52 is enough new prospective clients to keep you entertained for three lifetimes. Clients are not an "end", they are a means to an end. Simply bringing on a new client is no reason to celebrate. If you gain access to each clients' inner circle, then you have an exciting business.

Identify Your MVP's

Which brings us to our next point – understanding who are your Most Valuable Prospects (MVP's). Most entrepreneurs think their MVP's are elusive strangers in their respective city or market area when in fact they are the friends and family members of their existing clients. Is it possible that one of your most significant untapped opportunities is your inability to capitalize on each of your clients' inner circles?

Based on the fact that your clients will have significantly more persuasive impact on their friends and family than you ever will, you need a process to transform your clients into a sales team who will wave your flag! This will ensure that the moment a conversation between your client and any of his or her 52 friends, associates or family members turns to what you do, your client will brag about you. That said, are you satisfied with the degree of your refer-ability and the quality and quantity of endorsements you are currently attracting?

If you get nothing else from this book, we hope you get this – it is the core of our marketing and business development philosophy. We are referring to the **Loyalty Ladder**. We didn't invent it. It's been around for a long time. We've simply adjusted it for clarity and precision. And we are convinced that it will be tremendously helpful to you.

Envision a ladder with five rungs and every single person in your market area is on one of those five rungs. You are striving for something called conversion. Your objective is to get as many people as possible to the top of the ladder. Let's start at the bottom. The bottom rung on the ladder is for **Suspects**. A suspect is, frankly, anybody with a pulse. Anyone who can fog a mirror is a suspect. Will it give a business owner a good return on their investment of time, money, energy and lung capacity talking to suspects? Clearly not. But we see people all the time who mistake movement for achievement. Or, as Hemingway said, "Mistake motion for action." These people are very busy stirring the proverbial pot. But they've yet to figure out the distinction between a suspect and the next rung on the ladder, **Prospects**.

The difference between a suspect and a prospect is profound and we can sum up the difference with one word. This word is worth an MBA in marketing. The word is *pre-disposition*. It's another way of saying *self-motivated*. A prospect is somebody who has been motivated in advance of you ever talking to them. When it comes to prospects, you can't want it more than they do. Wouldn't it be great if every prospect you ever talked to already "wanted it", meaning they were already self-motivated? Motivating people is draining, it can be like pumping air into a leaky tire. True prospects are self-motivated. Your objective is to sift the prospects from the mass of suspects and, most importantly, give them a reason to contact you. This is what truly defines a prospect. They contact you or a client of yours calls you on their friend's behalf.

As we all know, there are two types of phone calls: inbound and outbound. Inbound is when *your* phone rings. You pick it up and it's one of your favorite clients calling you saying, "Look, I know you're busy and I don't even know if you're accepting new clients right now, but you've got to talk to my buddy." Does it get much better than that?

Or a complete stranger calls you up and says, "I was talking to my friend over the weekend and she told me I have to talk to you." Your goal is to increase the frequency of that type of inbound call.

The Law of Attraction

In our relationships with our consulting clients, we are constantly reminding them about the Law of Attraction. This is another of the immutable laws we refer to that affect us all. There are two ways to get new clients. You either chase them or attract them. Which do you think is more fulfilling? Chasing or attracting? Your clients can help make you extremely attractive to the marketplace, if you give them a reason and if you empower them with a process on how to do so.

It is for this reason that we are not big fans of out-bounding, also known as cold-calling. No doubt you're saddened to know we're not going to suggest you engage in cold-calling. We're not the biggest fans of this technique. Some people like it. Some people defend it and say, "What are you talking about? It's a great way to build a business." Sure. You can also cut down a tree with a hammer if you try hard enough or keep at it long enough. Any expenditure of effort will garner a return on investment. We, on the other hand, want you to maximize your return by employing the Law of Attraction. We'll expand on this for you when we reveal our referral process later on in the book. For now, let's get back to the Loyalty Ladder.

Once you've got your true prospects in sight, your MVPs, your next job is to convert those prospects into **Customers**. At the very least, you want them as customers. You may wonder what we mean by saying *"at the very least."* A profound difference exists between a customer and the next rung on the ladder – a **Client**. Some people use these terms – *client* and *customer* - interchangeably and to them it may all be semantics, but we're going to explain our definitions which hold true throughout this book. *Clients* are exclusive to you. They empower you fully. Every single thing they need that you provide, they empower you to deliver. Those are *clients. Customers?* They do a little bit of business with you, but they also do business with some of your competitors. Customers buy something, clients buy *into* something. Based on that, is there a chance that some of your clients are actually just customers? Do you have a compelling way to convey your full array of offerings in order to convert customers into clients? And can you position this approach as a service to your customers rather than as a benefit to you? In the Actions section of this book we are going to reveal to you the exact proven process our coaching and consulting clients and 8020Platform subscribers use to gain full empowerment from all of their clients.

Advocates - The Ultimate Clients

The last and most important rung on the Loyalty Ladder is reserved for **Advocates**. Don't get faked out by how many clients you've got. Some people talk about how many clients they have and they wear that number like a badge of honor. It really doesn't matter how many clients you've got. What is important is the number of *advocates* you have. That's where the value is. Advocates are people who think you walk on water. They feel great about your relationship, they trust you and are fiercely loyal. They wouldn't dream of doing business with anybody else. They are fully empowering. Best of all, they brag about you to anybody who'll listen. Think about the advocates you have now, perhaps you have five or ten. Based on the rule of 52, what would happen to your business if you had 150 advocates?

There is a practical component to this as well as an element of personal fulfillment. It takes far more time, money, effort and energy to convert a prospect into a customer or client than it does to convert a client into a referral generating advocate. That's just practical. But even more importantly, every year you are in business should be more fulfilling. The easiest way to achieve this is to stop trying to convince new people and instead work with people who are already convinced. Show them why, who and how they should be introducing people to you. Advocacy is all about why, who and how. Our proven referral process will enable you to "train", for lack of a better word, *why* your advocates should introduce people to you, *who* your advocates should introduce to you and *how* your advocates should introduce people to you. And best of all, this process positions referrals as a benefit to your advocates rather than as a favor to you. And that is extremely attractive to high-caliber individuals.

We're asking you to focus on the commitment of advocates rather than simply the commissions or income you earn from new clients. Stop trading your time for money. Focus instead on the lifetime value of relationships with advocates. Relationships can last long after you've spent the money.

We mentioned that we are going to reveal our referral process in the Actions section of the book, but for now let's get the wheels turning relating to the mindset of refer-ability. Earlier, we asked you to consider *why, who* and *how*. If we want more referrals, let's focus first on the *why*. The *why* speaks to purpose and the *how* speaks to process. When it comes to increasing the quality and quantity of referrals you receive, purpose is actually more powerful than process. In other words, when the *why* is clear, the *how* gets easier.

Position Advocacy as a Benefit to Clients, Not to You

So *why* should a client refer a friend to you? *Why* don't you get as many as you'd like? The answer is probably rooted in how you position referrals. Are referrals a service to your clients or a favor your clients do for you? Most people unknowingly position referrals as a favor or benefit to themselves. The problem with doing this is that you end up looking needy. We advise you to never bring your needs to your clients. It's not attractive. Ultimately the "favor" approach can stimulate referrals but we feel it actually hurts you more than it helps over the long run. Remember, it's not what you say but rather what they hear that really counts. When you ask for a referral because it will help you build your business, what does your client really hear? It creates an atmosphere of obligation rather than pure reciprocation and value.

Instead, take the position, and be sure to absolutely convince yourself, that it's a service you provide. You making yourself available to act as a sounding board, is a service to your clients and their close friends and family members. How much more attractive is it to say, *"As a value-added service to my clients, I make myself available to act as a sounding board. You might have a friend who asks you about me, or you might feel compelled to make an introduction to help someone out. If that happens I will make the time to offer objective advice that they can use to make an informed decision. It's a value-added service I offer to my best clients."* As opposed to saying, *"I'm trying to grow my business, do you know anyone who might need what I sell?"* In the Activities section we will disclose this process in its entirety.

Wouldn't it be great if your clients not only knew *why* they should refer some to you but also *who* is a good fit for you? And who you are good fit for? Do your clients think of you as a specialist who is all things to some people, or do they think of you as a generalist who tries to be all things to all people? In other words, do they know who they should be referring to you? Have you ever received a referral from a client and, after you met their friend, dreaded the idea of bringing them on as a new client but did so anyway because you didn't want to offend the client who sent the referral? Our process will help you communicate to your clients *who* they should be steering to you.

Furthermore, it will also help you provide your clients with a clear and precise process for *how* to actually make an introduction. We don't mean to leave you hanging, but the process we're referring to has been proven to work by our coaching and consulting clients over the last several years and will be provided to you in a turnkey fashion in the Actions section of the book. All of the scripting and templates are in the Actionable CD-ROM and are also drawn directly from our coaching curriculum.

Remember

- Empowerment and endorsements by clients must be positioned as a service to them rather than as a favor or benefit to you.

Take Action Now! *(Week 1)*

- Apply the Loyalty Ladder to your business and develop a mindset that has you and your team fixating on the value of advocacy.

Your Overlooked Vulnerabilities

Let's get back to the Strategic Analysis. We've talked about some of the untapped opportunities that exist within your business which include converting customers to fully empowering clients and then converting them to referral generating advocates. There is a tremendous array of upside that will come from that.

Now we have to discuss the issues that could be undermining your success and holding you back. This brings us to your potentially overlooked vulnerabilities. Whether or not you feel these issues are relevant to you right now, we want you to consider them as they are crucial for taking your business to the next level. But be proactive about it. You'd never wait for your oil light to come on in your car before you did something about it, would you? The issues we are about to discuss could address why your business is not firing on all cylinders.

The Importance of Organization and Structure

"The goal is to run your business so that it doesn't run you.
Paradoxically, this can only happen once you've made yourself obsolete.
When the day comes that you don't need to be present and your business
can still be productive, you are on the verge of a breakthrough."

– David Miller and Duncan MacPherson

The best description we have heard an entrepreneur use to explain his stalled business was simply, "I can't seem to do any more business but I absolutely can't afford to do any less."

Many business professionals find this to be true. Overall, their life is good. They earn a good living and have earned the right to be content. However, deep inside, ambition nags at them. They know they could break through the plateau. But they just can't seem to take their business higher. And, of course, they have a lifestyle to support and cannot allow their business to go any lower.

Ultimately, they can't work harder. Of course, they could work more hours, but the collateral damage to their personal lives would be unacceptable and would take them down the path of diminishing returns. Furthermore, fear of rocking the boat inhibits them. If it isn't really broken, why try to fix it? In other words, if they attempt to tinker with or re-engineer their current approach, they risk adjustments which might not lead to improvements or could possibly even set things back.

As one entrepreneur put it, "I can't afford to be right, *eventually*. My monthly expenses on both business and personal levels require results *right now*." This mindset results in people sticking with the status quo and maintaining a business which simply hovers.

So, you can't work any harder. And you're not prepared to resign yourself to "this is as good as it gets." What is the answer?

More often than not, one, two or all of the following three factors must be addressed in order to take your business to the next level, to evolve from *survive* to *thrive*.

Mistaking Motion for Action

When we ask a businessperson, "How are things?" nine times out of ten, the answer will be, "I've never been busier." Our response is always, "Busy doing what?" The Law of Cause and Effect states that your activities will determine your productivity. If you want your productivity to increase, the first place you should look is the activities you engage in which give you the best return on your investment of time and energy. Think about it. The Pareto Principle states that 80% of your productivity stems from about 20% of your activities. In other words, you make about 80% of your income every day in about an hour. So, what goes into that hour? Talking to and meeting with your favorite clients and the most predisposed prospective clients available to you. All other activities must support these two essential activities.

Unless you are a one-person operation, one of the most obvious ways to increase your capacity to do more of what you really get paid to do is to delegate as many supporting activities as possible.

For many entrepreneurs, managing people and all the accompanying hassles can be a big issue. Many perceive managing people as actually exacerbating the problem because it can be a distraction. Hiring new people adds yet another expense and could potentially upset the chemistry of the staff currently in place.

These concerns can be addressed if you step back and scrutinize your business. Determine whether it is truly built on predictable, sustainable and duplicable systems driven by accountability and consistency. Does everyone on your team know their job description? Do they follow predetermined systems and procedures, or are they left to their own devices?

We have seen many, many entrepreneurs with successful businesses supported by talented people but who unknowingly created self-imposed limitations because, frankly, everyone in the organization flew by the seat of their pants. Time after time, the creation of an

Organizational and Structural Chart followed by the refinement of systems outlined within a Procedures Manual has proven to be essential.

Systems Create Success

The Organizational Chart is simply a snapshot of everyone on your team with a brief description of what they do. One sheet of paper is required and, when completed, becomes the cover sheet of the Procedures Manual. Now if you have never done this before you may be wondering, "Is this worth the effort?" Time and time again, when conducting a Strategic Analysis for one of our coaching and consulting clients, we have determined that in order to develop a systematized business this is an essential step back in order to take several forward.

The Random House Dictionary defines *systems* as "a group or combination of things or parts forming a complex or unified whole." Does this sound like your business? Dry as it may be, it fits not only the dictionary definition, but is critical for your success.

Of particular interest in the definition is the word *unified*. If all the great things you may do in your business are not systemized, or perhaps you have marketing initiatives for some of your clients some of the time but not all the time, it's time to get serious about installing predictable, sustainable and duplicable systems. Many of our high-caliber coaching and consulting clients, as well as users of the 8020Platform got on the right track and realized significant business breakthroughs only after deploying an organization and structural chart for accountability and then, as you will see in a moment, integrating that within a procedure manual.

Take a good hard look at your operation. Would it continue to function like a Swiss watch if you weren't there all the time? Could you convince us, today, that your enterprise is a true business and not just simply a company that sells things? Have you created something with great value, predictable outcomes and ironclad systems? Could you provide documentation detailing exactly how to operate and run your business right down to the smallest detail?

If you have created a business with true systems, you probably already know the freedom and control it has brought to your business and personal life. The haphazard approach simply cannot compare. In the spirit of *beginning with the end in mind*, with true systems in place, you are most likely to achieve one of the following:

- the sale of your established business for a substantial profit
- the expansion or franchising of the proprietary approach you've created
- handing your business to the next generation or to a management team so you can take more time off

None of these scenarios can be realized fully unless, and until, systems are in place.

As an analogy, when driving a car with a standard gearshift in first gear longer than you should, you can almost hear the car breathe a sigh of relief as you shift into second and work your way up to 4th or 5th gear. How can it be that you're accelerating as you're expending less energy? Simply put, everything is just working more efficiently as you gain momentum. Your business should work that way as well. You work diligently and contribute much in the early stages of the business. With time, it should become less draining and start giving back to you.

So where do you start? If you are going to build a business based on systems, the first step is to clearly define each individual's responsibilities within your organization. You and your team have to sit down and determine who does what and when. On a daily basis, you and your team engage in proactive and reactive activities. Based on the Law of Cause and Effect, all of these activities effect your productivity. You and your team need absolute clarity of who is accountable for each of these activities. On the Actionable CD-ROM you will find an organizational and structural template which will allow you to create a panoramic snapshot of your business. Think of this as the hub, not only for accountability, but also for consistency.

Remember

- Your goal is to build a business that is productive whether or not you are present.

Take Action Now! *(Week 1)*

- Use the organization and structure template on the Actionable CD-ROM to ensure accountability and consistency.

The Creation and Benefits of a Procedure Manual

"Your business is supposed to serve your life,
not the other way around."

– Michael Gerber

The Procedure Manual is an extension of the organizational chart and is nothing more than documentation of how you and your team work. From the very mundane tasks, such as the various office supplies you have on hand at any given time as well as where you buy them and where you store them, to more sophisticated tasks such as your process for meeting with a prospective client for the first time, determining a fit and fast-tracking new clients to *advocate* status. We don't mean to oversimplify, but it's not as complicated as it sounds.

More often than not, when we raise this topic with one of our consulting clients, the immediate response is either, "this sounds like work" or "I can't really see the payoff here."

It **is** work. But you can have 80% of this done in the next two weeks. It can be done. We know. If you will take the templates in the Actionable CD-ROM in the back of this book and tell all your staff that over the next two weeks you want everyone to document their daily tasks, it will get done. And remember, *done* is better than *perfect*. (This stems from the countless times an entrepreneur-client of ours has called in a panic to tell us one of their key support people just gave two weeks notice – sure enough the manual got done before the departure and the new person took it and ran with it immediately.)

And this leads to the payoff issue. Actually, there are a number of payoffs here. First of all, consider the entrepreneurial paradox: you are truly successful the day you have made yourself obsolete. The day your business can run like a Swiss watch, everyday, without you there to oversee it - at that point you are really in a groove. And there is a definite distinction between being in a *groove* and being in a *rut*.

It is remarkably revealing when we ask an entrepreneur, "What would happen if you took a month off, starting tomorrow?" We have received a great many downright shocking and funny responses over the years. The most illuminating was, "The only thing scarier than that is the thought of what would happen if my assistant took a month off tomorrow. And I don't even really know what she does, but my clients love her."

It's one thing to say you have to be present for your business to be productive. But it's another vulnerability altogether to say that you are at the mercy of maverick talent. How much of a set-back would it be if one of your key staff members left in two weeks? We've seen the departure of one key person put a business owner into a 6-month rut. Can you imagine how powerful it would be if you hired a replacement, plugged the new person into your organizational chart and then handed him or her your procedure manual and said, "here is how we do things around here, just add water!'"?

More importantly, by creating what is essentially a franchise-ready business, a business with duplicable procedures, the value of your business will increase. If you were to sell your business, you could show your procedure manual to the suitor during the due diligence process and explain how he or she could easily replicate your success.

The manual ensures you are running the business instead of it running you. You could take more time off without worrying that it's all unraveling without you. You could expand with certainty and efficiency. Even if none of those benefits appeal to you consider this, you've given a lot to your business, it's time for the business to give a little back. This is the first step in that direction.

At this point, if we have drifted into completely foreign territory and you're wondering if there is an example of how this has actually benefited an entrepreneur, allow us to give you this one. Do you remember Ray Kroc's story? Ray Kroc sold milkshake makers and straws to restaurants in America. One day he walked into the original McDonald's Brothers' restaurant—back when they only had one arch! Way ahead of his time, Ray Kroc secured the international franchise rights for that restaurant. First thing he did, he documented everything into a binder. You know what they've done since then? They've sold that binder around the world more than 30,000 times. They put the pickles on the hamburgers in the exact same way in every restaurant in every city in every country around the world. There are no maverick hamburger makers left to their own devices, no one getting creative with the ketchup gun. This is just one of countless examples of entrepreneurs that propelled their businesses to completely new levels through the deployment of a procedure manual.

Let's say you really get ambitious and decide to expand your business, how powerful would it be if all new staff members were shown exactly how to do their jobs and be empowered by such clarity? That is pure scale-ability. They wouldn't have to re-invent the wheel or try to figure things out for themselves. It's no longer a mentor-protégé relationship; it is about authentic and predictable leverage. Accountability (ensuring staff members add to profits, not costs) and consistency (ensuring no deviations) becomes a certainty.

Remember

- Your procedure manual can be 80% done in two weeks and is essential to creating liberation and order in your business and your life.

Take Action Now! (Weeks 2 & 3)

- Use the Procedure Manual template on the Actionable CD-ROM to create your procedure manual.

Client Classification and a AAA Ideal Client Profile

"Growth is for Vanity - Profit and Progress are for Sanity."
— Entrepreneurial Truism

Are you focused on growth or progress? This issue affects us all and can make a business vulnerable. The entrepreneurial fallacy is *grow or perish*. The goal for many of us is not to see how big we can get, but rather, how small we can stay. Do you know your capacity? By that we mean, how many clients can your current infra-structure support before opportunity leakage and collateral damage creep in? Are you on a course of growth or progress? A business owner, referred to us by a client, said a few things which made us think. Fifteen minutes into the conversation we learned he was making a ton of money, had 900 clients, was building this colossal business and he had no life. He was stressed out, out of shape, he had stuff going on at home we couldn't believe he'd tell us and yet he said to us, "I've heard good things about you guys. I'm thinking about hiring you to help me *grow* my business." Our first reaction was to say, "The best thing we can help you do is dismantle this thing." Of course he was immediately defensive, "What are you talking about?" So we explained, "Listen, this track you're on is hurting you more than it's helping you. It's costing you more than it's getting you. You sound stressed." You know what he did to relieve stress? He went to Costco and bought a $59 water fountain which gurgled water in his office all day to create a relaxing atmosphere and he listened to Enya

CDs in his car on the way to and from work. (We couldn't make that up!)

He finally relented when we asked, "Do you have an ideal client profile? Who is your ideal client? Describe your ideal client. You are building your business a mile wide and an inch deep. You're all over the map." We cited that old adage, "It's more important to reach people who count than it is to count the number of people you're reaching." He was like the hunter who walked into the forest and randomly fired his rifle and said, "Let's see if something runs into that."

Getting Started

Think of your ideal client. What makes him or her meet that criteria? Remember, we didn't say best client. Most entrepreneurs describe an ideal client with a singular issue in mind - how much revenue does he or she generate for my business? It goes much deeper than that. We ask our clients to take a panoramic view when describing their ideal clients and we urge them to apply our Triple-A process.

The first A is simple. *Action.* To what degree does the ideal client take action with you to be considered a real asset? How much revenue does the action typically generate? Keep in mind, when you think about the ideal client we want you to think of the word *fit*. Your expertise and the solutions you provide are a perfect fit for whom? Define that person. As you will see, this becomes a tool that is very attractive to high-caliber clients in keeping with projecting a specialist approach.

The second *A* of the ideal client profile is *Attitude.* The ideal client has a great attitude. Even if a client is top of the action list, a lousy attitude can hurt more than help your business. It's a slippery slope made more slick by the infectiousness of his negative attitude. Think about it, the ideal client doesn't focus on what you cost, he focuses on what you're worth to him. Does the ideal client constantly question or malign your fees or pricing? Oscar Wilde was right when he said, "A cynic is somebody who knows the cost of everything and the value of nothing." The ideal client sees your value. He has a great attitude. What's his attitude about empowerment? Does your ideal client also deal with your competitors, really making him only a customer? To us, that is like going to one dentist to work on the top of your mouth and another dentist to work on the bottom? The ideal client has an attitude where they value empowering one professional in a specific area rather than dabbling with a collection of providers.

The third *A* is *Advocacy.* The ideal client is actually an advocate. They are fiercely loyal, fully empowering, a joy to work with, your team loves them and they brag about you to anybody who'll listen. Advocates appreciate the merits of *buying into* a relationship with a professional rather than simply *buying something* from a vendor.

Take a look at your client base and determine who meets your **Ideal Client Profile** or at least has the ability to in the near future. These are your Triple-A or AAA clients. Strive to clone them. Competitor-proof them. They are an asset. Protect it. Most of all, they deserve your attention. A great many people need you. However, it is an error in judgment to spend time with people who need you at the expense of people who deserve you. And remember the Law of Environment. This immutable law tells us that our favorite clients will live near, work with and refer people pretty much like themselves. Disregard the occasional exception and consider this law carefully, and not solely from an income perspective. There is a personal development issue here too. Don't just ask what you're getting from your business, also think about who you're becoming. Few things impact who we're becoming more than the people we're around on an ongoing basis.

Once you've identified your existing and prospective AAA clients, you then need to assign a classification for your remaining clients. Examples would be AA clients to describe a client who takes decent action and has good attitude yet never sends a referral (This could be a potential AAA with a little coaching). A single A client would describe someone who takes action but has a poor attitude and isn't an advocate. You could then create B, C, D clients to describe the degree of action these customers take. As you will see later on, this classification tool will be directly linked to your Client Service Matrix. This matrix will outline the degree of service each client receives. This is essential because virtually every business reflects the Pareto Principle – that again being – 80% of their business is generated by about 20% of their clients. The service matrix ensures that the most deserving 20% receive 80% of your time and attention.

Right-Sizing

"Never wrestle with a pig. You both get dirty, but the pig likes it."
– Ghandi

After you have established your ideal client profile, you have an important and perhaps difficult decision to make about your current clients who don't meet your profile. Do you keep them as clients, or not? Can they become advocates? Do lower value clients have an adverse affect on your capacity to serve newly attracted AAA clients? Do these people have too-high of a hassle factor on you and your team to be worth the effort?

Doubtless, some of these people have been with you since day one and others may be like family to you. (We would keep a client with a great attitude, occasional advocacy and low action.) But chances are there are some clients that should be jettisoned. You may be reluctant to part with the income they bring and you can make exceptions but be practical and realistic and try to step beyond emotion and sentiment.

In letting clients go, entrepreneurs often make another mistake. They *fire* some clients. The last thing any industry needs is business people firing clients. If you have too many clients or if they do not meet your profile, you are doing them – and yourself - a disservice by keeping them. Be professional and gracefully bow out of relationships where the chemistry is poor between you and your client or where the hassle factor is high.

Respectful Disassociation

When you have identified clients who aren't a good fit for you going forward, call each of them and take the high road with a forthright and rational approach such as the following.

> *"Until recently, I've been trying to be all things to all people. Over time, I found myself becoming a generalist. We've been bursting at the seams as a result and things are starting to fall through the cracks. Going forward, I've decided to become a specialist who strives to be all things to some people. I know my capacity, and in order to offer superior service, I have to make some changes to my business. Part of that includes using an ideal client profile which reflects the type of client who is a good fit for my team and me."*

At this point, elaborate upon your AAA criteria.

"Based on this profile and our history together, I feel there isn't a good fit going forward. However, as a service to you I have identified someone else I feel would be a better fit for you and I will make the introduction if you would like."

You will - frankly - be amazed at the outcome of this exchange. Either the client will agree and move on effortlessly or they will fight to stay on board with you. They'll say such things as, "It never occurred to me I should empower you fully." Or, "I can move everything to you." You may even hear, "I didn't know you were accepting new clients, but I can easily start referring people to you."

You can decide to keep the client on board, conditionally, if they agree to respect the rules of engagement, those rules being that they strive to become a AAA client. You didn't start your business with these rules, you have developed them and are only now telling your clients your expectations. Given the opportunity and a clear understanding of your new mandate, many of these people will gratefully evolve from being simply customers into being true advocates. They do so because you clearly explain why it matters and how they will benefit. In some instances your instincts will tell you the client is not really going to respond. Maintain your integrity. Some will try to convince you they can change, but when you sense they are simply paying lip service or if your instincts tell you to steer clear, be professional, but firm. Remember, actions can change, attitudes rarely do.

You: *I just don't think there is a good fit going forward.*

Client: *I can change, I didn't mean to be a pain to your people.*

You: *I just don't think there is a good fit, but I'll introduce you to …*

Client: *But I don't want to work with anyone else.*

You: *I appreciate that, but based on the direction I'm taking, I just don't think there is a good fit here.*

The point of right-sizing is to build a clientele comprised exclusively of people with whom you want to work. These are the clients who will turn into flag wavers and sing your praises to their friends, family and associates. These clients are the key to building a successful, profitable business which gives you time to enjoy the things which matter to you.

Remember

- The clients who generate 80% of your revenue deserve 80% of your time. This group rarely exceeds 20% of your clientele.

Take Action Now! *(Week 2)*

- Create a AAA Ideal Client Profile using the template in the Actionable CD-ROM.

Build Client Chemistry with FORM

"Chemistry with your clients is just as important as your credentials and competencies as a business professional."
— Duncan MacPherson and David Miller

When we work with an entrepreneur on an individual consulting basis, we strive to help him or her create a code-of-conduct that creates long-term client relationships built on trust. There are three core elements that create trust: Consistency, Congruency and Chemistry. We call them The Three C's of Advocacy. *Consistency* states that you follow procedures and systems with unwavering precision and accountability. *Congruency* states that you always do what you say with accuracy and integrity. *Chemistry* states that you develop a meaningful rapport with your clients. By creating an organizational and structural chart integrated with a procedures manual, you will achieve consistency. By maintaining a forthright consultative approach you will create congruency. But focusing solely on those two is not enough. Creating chemistry with clients goes a long way towards insulating you from external issues and making you less vulnerable. So, how do you create chemistry?

Think about your client conversations. Clients reveal things to you that go beyond what they are buying from you. Do you capture and chronicle that information? The following is a proven process that enables you to invest every conversation with a client into the rest of the relationship and in the process build chemistry and trust by showing each client that you are interested in them. It may sound trite, but it's just as important that you be interested as it is to be interesting. That interest in your clients builds chemistry and chemistry builds trust.

An easy way to achieve that is to create **FORM** profiles for each of your AAA clients. FORM is an acronym that represents the four key components to a typical client relationship. Strive to bring value to all four.

The *F* in *FORM* stands for *Family*. Learn everything you possibly can about the families of your AAA clients and capture this information in a profile that you and your team can refer to and then look for ways to bring value in this area in the future. The following is an example of the power of understanding a client's family and paying attention to their concerns. One of our favorite consulting clients came to us in a very somber, dark mood. Of course we asked, "What's up?" He proceeded to tell us that something dreadful had happened to one of his client's family members. This client had come to him and bared his soul. "He told you that?", we couldn't help but ask. "That says a lot about your relationship. It's a moment of truth and certainly defines your relationship. What are you going to do?" Our client said, "I don't know." "You *have* to respond to this," we advised. "Buy the book, *When Bad Things Happen to Good People*, and send it to your client with a card saying something like

'Thinking about you, it's a tough time, call me if you just need to chat.' " His client called a few days later to say that it was the most thoughtful thing anybody had done. Are we advising you to be in the gift-giving business? No. We are recommending you look for ways to show your clients that you're paying attention. We'll give you more ideas on this later.

O stands for *Occupation.* Know what your AAA clients do. Learn to understand their business. Be aware of their trials, tribulations and triumphs and look for ways to bring value to them in this area. Again, when a circumstance arises that merits your attention, respond in a meaningful manner.

R is for *Recreation.* Every one of us integrates goal-achieving activities and tension-relieving activities into day-to-day living. When your clients talk about their hobbies and recreational interests, listen carefully. Make notes and look for ways to bring value in these areas.

Of course, the *M* stands for your *Message.* The products and services you sell and the solutions or expertise you provide are your message. You are the messenger. When a prospective client meets you for the first time, what do they really buy? Are they connecting with your message or with you, the messenger? When your best client waves your flag to a friend, what does that client spend more time bragging about? The message or the messenger? When a client leaves you and goes to a competitor, why do they leave? Is it due to some kind of disconnect between them and the messenger or dissatisfaction with the message? We will never trivialize what you deliver, in terms of the message. But the message is probably not proprietary. And bringing good value in terms of your message is expected. Doing a good job in that department is not guaranteed to exceed their expectations. Delivering your message with quality is essential but paying attention to the other areas of the client's life shows that you are striving to exceed expectations. We'll say it again, if you want to competitor-proof your clients, gain their full empowerment and improve your refer-ability, it comes down to one word. Trust. The Three C's must be in place.

It's one thing to know your AAA client inside out, it's another thing to create a system and process to ensure that information is really serving you well. By this point in your relationships with your AAA clients, you already know a great deal about them. If you're like most entrepreneurs we know, you keep this incredibly valuable information in your head. Let's just back up a few steps and reconsider a *predictable, sustainable and duplicable system*. If this information about your most valuable asset - your AAA clients - is in your head, it's definitely not an intellectual property. And it is most definitely not something your team can use if you're not present.

Some entrepreneurs trivialize this concept and feel that simply delivering a good product or service is enough. Again, your solutions and services are not enough to be considered a Unique Selling

Proposition (USP). And we'll say this again too, it is a given that you deliver good solutions, but your competitors are continually trying to best you in that regard, thus making your solutions more commoditized each and every day. The one thing your competitors cannot do, with as much success as you, is develop chemistry with your clients. Your clients do not and will not reveal nearly as much information to a competitor courting them as they will to a trusted provider such as you are, or can be. Our best advice to any business professional who has hit a plateau and is looking to take his or her business to the next level is simply this: get to know everything you can about your best clients and chronicle the information within a system. Whether you use our 8020Platform or some other CRM or even just simple file-folders, you must have an integrated mechanism which transforms everything a client reveals to you into an invaluable, actionable, intellectual property.

Think about it. In a typical 20-minute conversation with a great client, you talk about his family, his business, his recreational interests and - of course - your message: the solutions and services you provide.

The family, occupation and recreation information can be incredibly valuable. Relationships become stronger every time a client reveals something not related to business. These are *moments of truth*. And when a client reveals something personal, he is essentially saying, "I trust you."

Here are some examples to help set your gears in motion. We'll get into this in more detail in the Actions section of the book but first consider the following.

One of your best clients informs you he and his wife just had a baby. Do you enter the event into your client profile and send a small thoughtful gift, like a Baby Einstein educational DVD and card, to congratulate them?

Again, we're not suggesting you get into the gift-giving business. If you're creative and imaginative, build your own solutions to address recognition and praise and everything else you deem appropriate in honoring your clients' confidences. Sometimes a meaningful moment of truth with a client justifies a response of some kind. It's more important to be thoughtful than it is to spend a lot of money.

If you send a small gift to pay tribute to a milestone of some kind - birthday, anniversary or meaningful achievement - ensure what you send has both impact and shelf life. *Impact* denotes something personalized which speaks to them. The information you captured with FORM can guide you in that regard. This initiative is value-added, but it's only valuable if it's something the client actually values. Something with *shelf life* simply means something which sticks around for a while.

Moments of truth will be numerous, varied and endless. As your relationships with your clients unfold, grow and develop, you will undoubtedly find not only personal enrichment but also a great deal of satisfaction, to say nothing of increased income, in responding to those moments with consideration, respect and a bit of imagination.

A client tells you he'll be embarking on a substantial vacation to Asia. Why not send an email with a few links to informational websites featuring the cities the client mentioned?

You taste a terrific, new wine at the local wine festival. You think of a great client, with whom you've just celebrated a 10 year business anniversary with, and who also appreciates fine wine. Why not pay tribute with a thank you card, a nice corkscrew and a bottle of this new wine?

These Fundamental Strategies Make This Approach Effective:

1. Be targeted. This may be difficult to do with every client and every moment of truth. At the very least, start with your best and favorite AAA clients. They are the most deserving. They bring the most value to your business. They take Action on a consistent basis, have a great Attitude and are predisposed to Advocacy.

2. Make it a habit. The FORM process must become part of your day-to-day code-of-conduct and become habitual.

3. Be unique. Develop your own recognizable style, something you do for your clients, something out of the ordinary, something memorable. For example, send Thanksgiving cards every year to say, "Thanks for a great relationship!" (That is also a time when they are with family members – potentially great MVP's!) It's unique and exceeds the client's expectations because virtually no one does it.

4. Be consistent. Trust is broken when your client's expectations of you are not met. If you are all over the map, randomly dabbling at things, you'll be conspicuous by your lack of consistency.

Get On It!

Many business people hear about the FORM concept and say to themselves, "This is a good idea, I should do this." A week later, nothing has happened. The Law of Diminishing Intent kicked in and the status quo prevails. The best are separated from the rest in business because the best understand that a good idea not implemented is worthless. We'll discuss this in more detail in the Reality Check section. In the meantime, keep in mind, the best set out to make good ideas habitual by creating a process. They strike while the proverbial iron is hot and translate a good idea into results quickly. They also empower their teams to use their judgment to execute the process.

Consider the following information and strive to document as much as you can for all AAA clients in these categories:

Family

- The Usual Suspects: names, ages, birthdays of all immediate family members (send cards)
- Children's school placement, semester, fast-tracking, university program (send graduation gifts)
- Children's milestones: first jobs, driver's license (recognition gifts to child)
- Children's activities: sports, competitions, dance, music (recognition to child)
- Children's holiday plans: i.e. camps (information articles)
- Family pet(s): type, name, age, breed, specific problems, kenneling, rates (everyone loves talking about their pet).

In paying attention to the next generation, you are, as Confucius said, "Digging your well before you're thirsty."

Occupation

- Job promotion (congratulatory gift)
- Job loss or business set back ("You'll land on your feet!" card)
- Community service recognition (congratulatory gift)
- Moonlighting activities (information articles if client is exploring a possible future line of work, like teaching)
- Volunteer activities (partnering or fundraising with clients'

chosen organization)

- Duplicate all of the above for spousal inquiries

Recreation

- Type of holiday property owned and location (fix-up articles)
- If holiday property is paid off (asset management)
- Whether holiday property is used as rental income source (tax articles)
- Recreational activities engaged in (subscription to specialty magazines)
- Travel holidays planned (interest articles)
- Leisure activities of client (special event invitations)
- Health related: broach health topics only when a client raises the issue in response to a "How are things in general?" question. But if you learn a client has quit smoking, send a congratulatory card/gift with words of encouragement.
- Duplicate all of the above for spousal inquiries

Message

- Anything and everything that relates to the products and services you provide

Remember

- Be targeted, habitual, unique and consistent.

Take Action Now! *(Week 4)*

- Use the FORM Client Profiling Tool in the Actionable CD-ROM and begin to deploy it with your AAA clients.

Section 2: Targets and Goals

"Invest Your Past Into the Future."

– Jim Rohn

The Strategic Analysis step in our STAR approach is essentially designed to help you look back and make critical observations about your business. The Targets and Goals step is designed to help you look forward. We get excited talking about this concept because this exact process has not only been helpful for a variety of our clients, it's also helped us in achieving meaningful goals ourselves.

Success is Achieved by Design, Not By Chance

We can face the future in one of two ways: with anticipation or with apprehension. How do we face the future with *anticipation?* We design it.

Having goals enables us to see past obstacles, to get back up when we stumble, helps us focus on how and where we want to go and prevents us from drifting off the path. We all drift. It's natural because of the distractions and external issues and interruptions that occur on a daily basis. We get faked out and sometimes become lulled into ignoring the track we should be running on. Clearly set goals rejuvenate us and restore our enthusiasm. Additionally, by setting goals, we're reminded that we must be nimble and adaptable and the game plan we rely on must be flexible to account for Murphy's Law. Where you want to go won't necessarily change; how you get there, however, may change. Our goals pull us back on track.

This is a critical benefit to the goal setting process and we say this based on personal experiences. We know first hand that your trajectory determines your destination. We can both recall Jim Rohn, the legendary personal development guru saying that, "The winds of opportunity blow the same for everybody. The difference is in how you set your sails to harness the wind." Your plan is the set of the sail that will take you to your goals.

Remind yourself that true success is incremental. It takes time. It builds slowly. Having goals enables us to build the bridge as we cross it because we know what's on the other side. We can go with confidence and courage because we know where we're going. You'll need to make mid-course corrections along the way but in the process you will also make meaningful and measurable progress in a very reasonable period of time.

Goals Are The Why - Your Purpose; Strategy Is The How - Your Process. Purpose Is Just As Important As Process.

Consider the full spectrum when you go through this exercise. If we asked ten businesspeople their goals, nine of the ten focus on only one aspect. Money. Don't misunderstand us. Money isn't everything, but it ranks up there with oxygen. Make as much money as you can. However, money doesn't make us valuable. The goal is not to see how much we get. The goal is to keep an eye on who we are becoming. We all know this to be important and true. Think about it. Have you heard the old expression? *Every life is either a warning or an example.* We've all met some rich warnings.

If you are like most businesspeople we meet, you've been to countless goal-setting seminars and read a variety of books on the subject. This brief exercise is not intended to replace any process or technique you currently employ. It is merely designed to enhance it.

Our perceptions, wants and desires change constantly. Goals are not always static. Goals can and should evolve with our ever-increasing awareness. Therefore, make it part of your ongoing business planning process to revisit this approach every 6 to 12 months. At that point, you may look back at what you recorded today and realize these thoughts are no longer representative of your current goals. You may want to amend your objectives, even slightly, to accommodate changes in your life. Sometimes achieving a goal can actually be anticlimactic. In that case, you have to be more impressed by how you achieved it and what it revealed in you than by the acquisition of the actual goal itself.

The greater your awareness and understanding, the greater the impact you will have in attaining your ideal life. After all, goals are written on paper, not in stone.

When doing this exercise, be open to ideas which encompass all aspects of your life. Financial goals are important but are often not achieved if not accompanied by some lifestyle objectives. Most people are motivated by the things which come with having money: free time, travel, fine dining, a new house or the benefits for family and community. Don't hesitate to include any and all goals and objectives from all facets of your life.

Remember: going through this process is what's important. It is proven that those who set goals, and believe in them, achieve more. If you have a map of where you are going you are more likely to get there. And if you change your mind about where you're going, you can easily re-plot your course.

Something to Think About

Consider the following questions: (Print these questions from the Actionable CD-ROM and spend some time writing out your answers.)

1) What three things of which you are especially proud did you accomplish last year?

All of us have achieved something meaningful. Look back for a moment and savor that. The pace of business today doesn't allow us a great deal of time to sit back and reflect. Perhaps you overcame some adversity or achieved a meaningful milestone through your resilience. You've heard the old maxim, *Circumstances don't make the man, they reveal him*. Adversity is a way better coach than success. We all love hearing stories of entrepreneurs who overcome adversity. As business consultants, we've often seen that it was a moment of adversity that revealed true greatness in a client while prosperity concealed it. None of us can deny, however, talking about adversity is much easier after we've overcome it. All experiences either hurt us or serve us. Adversity can serve us when we account for it and reflect on our accomplishments. Whatever you've accomplished last year, and we're sure there are some great things, take a few moments to remind yourself. It is a big deal.

2) Write seven things on your 5-year wish list?

Do you want to sell your business? Do you want to take more time off? We have some clients who take 4 months off a year. (We're not sure if you're into that kind of thing but it certainly works for them!) Perhaps you want to expand your business? Maybe you want to get into great shape? Write it all down. And don't stop at seven. Write as much as you like. Where do you want to go? What do you want to do? What do you want to achieve? What do you want to become? How much do you want to make? It's all important and, as we have stated, consider the full spectrum of what's important to you.

3) Identify three things on your list you feel you can achieve in the next 12 months.

Here is where you start to narrow your focus on what is achievable on a more immediate basis. As you go through your business plan these 12 month goals should be included where appropriate.

4) Identify the one item on your list which will have the most impact on your life.

This becomes your beacon. Take that beacon and ask yourself *why*. Why is that one item important? It's true, when the *why* is clear, the *how* gets easy. What is the strength of your *why*? You're reading this book to learn *how*. How can you competitor-proof your clients?

How can you gain their empowerment? How can you increase your refer-ability? How can you get your business to serve your life, instead of the other way around? While doing this exercise don't forget the *why*. This is where leadership emerges.

Norman Schwarzkopf gives a great seminar on leadership. He said, "When it comes to leadership, people always follow character first, strategy second." We'll never trivialize your strategy, the *how* of your business. The character - who you are and the person you've become - is the *why*. The *why* is a primary reason your team works with you toward your goals and the major reason your clients choose you. This mindset also keeps you focused on your legacy. We understand that not everyone gets as excited about this as we do and we also know that countless people have achieved great things without going through a goal setting process. Fair enough. We also know that everyone at some point has to ponder one of the two "coulds" in life. What "could be" or what "could have been". Goals give us anticipation and focus and serve us well to minimize regrets.

Again, you have given a lot to your business, it's time for your business to give a little back. The entrepreneurial precept is true - your business is supposed to serve your life, not the other way around. By regularly taking the time to go through this exercise and answer these questions you will re-focus your activities on what's important to you, determine what success means to you and ensure that you achieve it.

Remember

- Go through a goal setting exercise at regular intervals in your life and include these questions for clarity and perspective.

Take Action Now! *(Week 4)*

- Print the Goal Setting Worksheets from the Actionable CD-ROM and take the time to answer the questions.

Section 3: Actions - Your Business Development Activities

Establishing a Client-Centered Code-of-Conduct using DART

"Excellence is a habit not an act. We are what we repeatedly do."

– Aristotle

When you go through the Target and Goal Setting process, a major portion of your wish list will undoubtedly reflect your productivity goals. Now it is time to identify the specific activities that will make your productivity objectives become a reality.

The Law of Cause and Effect reminds us that if we want our productivity levels to increase, we must consistently be implementing the activities that garner the greatest return on our investment of effort. It bears repeating, 80% of your productivity stems from 20% of your activities. Most entrepreneurs make about 80% of their income, every day, in about an hour. 20% of your productivity comes from about 80% of your activities. We're not trivializing those activities, they're important, everything matters and everything you do affects everything else. The key however, is to focus on the activities that matter most.

We are continually reminding our coaching and consulting clients to be unreasonably time and capital efficient, with a particular emphasis on time. We say this because contrary to the old cliché, time is NOT money. Time is much more valuable than money. You can make more money but all of us have just 24 hours in a day. When you spend your time, it's gone. Being mindful of this is what gives effective entrepreneurs the winning edge. They are unreasonable with how they invest their time. And the winning edge, if you need reminding, suggests that the disparities in abilities between the best and the rest are often very small. The disparities in rewards however, between the best and rest are huge. You see it in all walks of life. A great example of this is professional sports. The winner of a golf tournament plays four rounds of golf and wins a million dollars. When you break it down, based on cause and effect, if that golfer averaged 70 shots per round, for a total score of 280, it means he made close to $3,600 every time he hit the golf ball. Not bad. Look at the leader board for #10 on the list. #10 made about $100,000. Was #1 ten times better than #10? Clearly not. #10 averaged about 72 shots per round, over four days, which means only 8 strokes separated the two players. #10 however made close to $350 per shot. Still not bad but compared to the winner the productivity was dramatically different. Like the winning athlete, top entrepreneurs are not ten times smarter, they don't work ten times harder, they don't spend ten times more on marketing. They have the winning edge and we are convinced it starts here.

Establish a Client-Centered Code-of-Conduct Using DART

When we work with an entrepreneur in the area of activities, our first goal is to help him or her establish a code-of conduct. A code-of-conduct is simply a predetermined array of habits that the entrepreneur relies on daily. There is a profound difference between being disciplined and habitually doing what's important. Like money, good habits compound and ultimately ensure your success.

At the end of a seminar we conducted a while back, a very professional and soft-spoken financial advisor approached us and spoke about how refreshing it had been to hear us talk about the importance of developing good habits. He'd found other *fancy* marketing strategies produced, at best, modest results. He then handed us a small booklet distributed by the National Association of Insurance and Financial Advisors in Washington, D.C. The booklet was the transcript of a speech presented by Albert Gray at the 1940 National Association of Life Underwriters convention. The title of the speech was The Common Denominator for Success.

We read the booklet. Mr. Gray's first point struck a chord. The author described the impact of realizing the secret he was trying to discover lay not simply in what men and women did to be successful but also in what made them do it. He came to understand the secret of success lies in habits formed. Successful people habitually do things unsuccessful people don't like to do.

As business development consultants we have seen first hand those achieving success in business have developed and consistently practice simple habits and rituals. They stay true to those habits long enough for the results to compound and take on a life of their own.

The following concept is a time-tested framework for developing a professional code-of-conduct. As you can tell, we're big on acronyms. We like them because they package a concept neatly, are thought provoking, and, best of all they are memorable. The acronym here is the word DART. Each of the four letters in DART represents a cornerstone to your professional code-of-conduct.

Deserve

The *D* in DART is the foundation of it all. The *D* stands for *deserve*. It sounds trite but every single thing you want your client to do, you must deserve. Do you *deserve* their loyalty? Do you *deserve* their empowerment? Do you *deserve* their endorsements? If you're in the knowledge-for-profit business such as consulting you have to ask yourself, do I *deserve* the fees I charge? In other words, "Am I fee-worthy?"

Look at the word *deserve*. If you draw a line between the first *e* and the *s* you are reminded that the word originates from the Latin words *to serve*. An unwavering commitment by you and your team to impeccable proactive and reactive client service is the foundation to achieving client loyalty, empowerment and endorsements.

Create a Service Matrix

The first step in taking your service deliverables to the next level is in creating a service matrix. Sit down with your team and list out all of your client service deliverables. Include everything - call rotations, newsletters, review meetings, planning sessions. Include every single form of service you provide, right down to sending Thank You cards. Use the template in the Actionable CD-ROM to get the process started. It is an incredibly revealing process and you and your team will probably be amazed when you see everything you do listed out on a sheet of paper.

Beside that list, make a column for accountability. Who takes care of each of those services? Who does it? Put the initials of the person responsible for implementation next to the task itself. For instance, if you are a consultant and you have a meeting with a perspective client, do you confirm that meeting yourself? When was the last time your dentist called you to confirm your dental appointment? Did the dentist call, or did the receptionist? The column is about accountability and serves as a gentle reminder to ensure that you focus on your core activities and only on the activities that are the best use of your time. Based on the Pareto Principle you should be performing about 20% of the tasks while your team is performing the remaining 80%.

Incidentally, this service matrix will integrate with your organizational chart and procedure manual. Beside the accountability column, you have a column dedicated to your AAA clients. As you can imagine, AAA clients get a check mark for every service deliverable you provide. They deserve it. In your enlightened self-interest AA clients, single A clients and every other client classification you have should not necessarily receive the same level of service as AAA clients do. There isn't enough time in the day to try to be all things to all people.

Furthermore, by not delineating the service you are providing based on client classification, here's the risk you run. The 80% of clients who generate 20% of your revenue will end up doing most of the referring. Now there are exceptions to every rule, but in all likelihood, these clients tend to refer people pretty much like themselves. Consequently, you end up growing your business based strictly on the number client relationships you have rather than the quality. If your goal is to replicate your AAA clients, you must blanket them with 80% of your attention. To punctuate this point, the service matrix is designed to ensure that you never spend excessive time with the 80% of your clients who generate 20% of your revenue at the expense of your most deserving 20% - especially your AAA clients. We're not being harsh or elitist, we're simply asking you to guard your time.

Stir the Pot with a 90-Day Call Rotation

Incidentally, at the very top of your list of service deliverables for AAA clients must be *The 90-Day Call Rotation*. Simply put, if you have 107 existing and potential AAA clients right now, it means that you will be calling two or three of them every business day over the course of the next 90 days. This is an absolutely essential habit to create and stick with.

You aren't calling to be the bearer of any profound news nor are you trying to sell anything. You are simply touching base with your favorite clients to demonstrate that you appreciate them and are thinking about them. As you are speaking with each of them, you have his or her FORM profile open and you are investing the conversation into the rest of the relationship. If you have good chemistry with the client, chances are that in a 20-minute conversation, 15 minutes will be focused on their Family, Occupation and Recreational interests with just a few minutes focused on your Message.

We could parade a number of entrepreneurs through your office who would tell you, "The call rotation is what I really get paid to do." We have a client on the West Coast who starts his day very early and wraps each day up at about 2:00 pm and takes every Friday off. The place runs like a Swiss watch. As he leaves each day, one of his assistants holds up a sheet of paper with the names of two clients and their numbers. He calls them from the car on his way home. He says, "Half the time they're not even there so I just leave a voice mail." What does he say to them? "Hey, how's it going, thinking about you." And using his FORM information he makes an inquiry or two. Half the time his clients call him back thanking him for calling. He says, "Half the time

I'm sitting in my driveway for 20 minutes talking to a great client." How much time does he spend talking about his message? "Almost never," he said. "Very little. It's mostly family, occupation, recreation." It's simple. It's powerful. And it's easy to do. But if it's so simple, so powerful and so easy to do, why doesn't everybody do it? Because it's easier not to do it. It's easy to think there are more important things to do. But nothing could be more important that consistently reaching out to touch base with your AAA clients. If you don't, you run the risk of essentially saying that you take your AAA clients for granted. Remember the old saying, "Absence makes the heart grow fungus." You're conspicuous by your absence and in the process your ability to competitor-proof your clients, gain their full empowerment and stimulate good referrals is undermined. Incidentally, if you have the capacity, it's not a bad idea to empower your team to contact select AA, A and other clients as part of a call rotation to try to convert them to AAA status.

Remember

- Strive to be all things to some people – those some people are your AAA clients.

Take Action Now! (Week 5)

- Use the templates in the Actionable CD-ROM to create your own Service Matrix and to make the Call Rotation habitual.

Ask

Asking Starts the Receiving Process

O nce you are on track in terms of creating and deploying a service matrix you will have put the odds in your favor so that you will *deserve* client loyalty, empowerment and endorsements. You then have to move to the A in DART which stands for *Ask*. Everything you want your clients and prospective clients to do, you must *ask* them. But here is the caveat, based on creating a professional code-of-conduct, you must examine how you *ask* them. Business owners who chase clients ask differently than business owners who attract clients. We want you to attract high-caliber clients and therefore we are asking you to closely scrutinize all the ways you *ask* people to do things.

A great place to start is to ask key AAA clients to attend a Client Advisory Council (CAC). This proven and incredibly revealing process enables you to do a "state of the nation" in terms of getting feedback on your overall approach. If you want to improve the way you deliver things, *ask* the people at the receiving end of what you deliver. Mark Twain said it best, "A customer is the only critic whose opinion really counts." So **ask** them how you are doing.

Before we give you an overview for how to implement a CAC, keep in mind that the entire turnkey process can be found in the Actionable CD-ROM. Everything you'll need to get your group together, what to say when they are together with you and how to say thanks after the session has taken place, can be implemented in a sequential and predictable manner.

The stories we could tell you are staggering. One client we proposed this to was initially quite skeptical but eventually agreed to try it. We said, "Make a list of your 15 favorite clients. If you had to give all your clients away and were allowed to keep only 15, who would they be? Call them up." And he just called them up and said. "I take my business very seriously but I don't want to get complacent. I know I can always raise the bar and the best way to do that is to ask the people who receive our service. Next Saturday I'm getting together with a small group of my clients and I will ask you all an array of important questions. Your feedback will be crucial to me and will strive to take action on it as soon as possible" He called 15, and 14 were flattered. One was going to be out of town. He got together with these 14 people for the planned one-hour meeting. Three hours later he was blown away. He asked them all the questions provided in the agenda within our process. For example, he asked this question about refer-ability (question #7 on our agenda). He said, "Have I earned the right for you to feel comfortable and confident enough to introduce a friend or family member to me? Yes or no?" One of his clients said to him, "I didn't even know you took referrals." He didn't actually ask for a referral. He just put it out there, just communicated it and it opened a very important dialogue about the concept of referrals. (As you will see, this is a huge philosophical departure in our approach as compared to others – you don't need to ask for referrals, just communicate that you accept them in a professional and attractive manner.)

Anyway, his client advisory council cost him a few hundred dollars. Big spender! He did it in his boardroom, provided donuts and coffee and gave everybody a pen. He was so blown away at the reaction, he did another one less than a year later. This one cost him about $2,200. In his boardroom, he had a follow-up conversation and he told them, "Here's what's happened since we had our meeting, here's the adjustments we've made. Thank you." After a 2-hour meeting they were all then whisked away to the Sky Dome in Toronto for a baseball game. He was so completely amazed at the now-advocate status of these 14 people that he was inspired to take the third session to an even higher level. The third client advisory council cost him $10,000. He rented a bed and breakfast in Niagara Falls for a weekend and invited the CAC members and their significant others. He spoiled them all rotten. He said, "The money's a drop in the bucket when you consider how much business has been generated by my Board of Directors, as I now call them."

Some business owners worry about opening the door to negative feedback about themselves. Frankly, given these are your best clients with whom you have good relationships, you'd already know if they had anything less than favorable feelings for you. But it is a common concern. Some seem to think their top clients have simply been dying for this chance to assemble a lynch-mob and walk away with their business en masse.

We have sat in on many CACs. Let us share with you what we've witnessed more than a dozen times. When your clients arrive, they are clear about the agenda. They know you want to hear from them how you can improve your service. They understand you think their opinion/perspective is important and worthy. When your clients show up they are already somewhat impressed.

The CAC is not a gimmick or a trick. Quite the opposite in fact. You are trying to communicate your philosophy as effectively as you can and to be completely open with your clients. You are essentially telling them, "This business is wonderfully challenging. It's fun, I love it. I love meeting and helping people exactly like you reach their business goals. Help me get a clear understanding of what people like you expect and value. I will consider everything you tell me, and if it can be implemented, I'll do it."

Your first CAC is the proverbial tip of the iceberg. It is imperative your council understands you wish to meet with them at least two, perhaps three times over the course of the next 24 months.

Remember

- Make your clients the voice you listen to. No one can offer better advice for taking your business to the next level than the members of your client advisory council.

Take Action Now! *(Week 6)*

- Customize the turnkey Client Advisory Council campaign and templates found in the Actionable CD-ROM.

Asking People to Move Up Your Loyalty Ladder

"You're not asking people to buy things from you, you are asking them to buy-into a lifelong relationship."

– Duncan MacPherson and David Miller

The Client Advisory Council, at the very least, will be invaluable for enabling you to ask your clients how you are doing. In the process your ability to competitor-proof your clients will increase. You now need to shift gears to determine how you can:

• Ask prospective clients to do business with you
• Ask existing customers to become fully empowering clients
• Ask clients to become referral generating advocates

Let's talk for a moment about how you deal with prospective clients. When a prospective client actually decides to do business with you and comes on board, who views that as an accomplishment? Do you view is as an accomplishment because you closed the sale or do they view it as an accomplishment because they qualified to work with you? For 9 out of 10 entrepreneurs, they are the ones celebrating when a new customer comes on board. Nowhere in the process does the prospect have to convince the entrepreneur that there is a good fit. The entrepreneur is doing all of the convincing.

Before you dismiss this concept, let us remind you that there is a profound difference between salesmanship and stewardship. Salespeople focus on the transaction and sell primarily the message while consultative professionals focus on the relationship and sell the benefits of the messenger. It is for this reason that we tell our coaching and consulting clients NOT to attempt to "close the sale" when they meet a prospective client for the first time. Think about it. The hidden agenda of most sales-driven businesspeople who meet prospective clients for the first time is to try to close them. We say, "have no hidden agenda" and here is why.

Your goal is to conduct yourself in a manner that contrasts your approach favorably to his or her current provider. That favorable contrast does not come from your ability to close them using salesmanship, as counterintuitive as that may sound. You, in fact, actually have three goals when meeting with a prospective client for the first time. If you achieve these three goals you will dramatically increase your persuasive impact over that of a salesperson.

Goal #1: Validation. When you meet a prospective client who's been introduced to you by an existing client, at the very least you want that prospect to go back to your existing client and validate the introduction, informing the existing client he or she was right to recommend you. What has just happened? The referral tap has been turned on, flat out. Your existing client will continue to refer you.

Goal #2: Contrast. As mentioned a moment ago, as the prospect is engaged in a conversation with you, he or she is comparing your approach to the other approaches they have encountered. As they start contrasting you favorably, they become predisposed to wanting to do business with you. This leads to the all important third goal.

Goal #3: Self-Motivation. When a prospective client meets with you for the first time, a combination of two emotions exist: anticipation and apprehension. The anticipation exists because they are thinking of the upside that could come from making a switch or all the benefits that could come from taking action. If they were referred to you obviously they heard good things about you and they want to believe that the comments are true and accurate. The apprehension stems from their fear of making a bad decision, fear of change and of course, fear of being sold. People today are naturally skeptical and guarded when they meet with a new vendor or service provider for the first time because past experiences tell them the hidden agenda of that person is to sell them something. So if that fear exists, why feed it? With our process, you will literally see the apprehension melt away as the prospective client realizes you are a consultative professional.

Here is the process:

Step 1 – Always Use an Agenda

After the pleasantries of the initial meeting, slide a formal agenda across the table (there are samples on the Actionable CD-ROM).

This powerful tool tells the person that you value his or her time and that you have a process to follow. As you will see in the templates, the agenda has the prospective client's name as well as the date and time of the meeting. It is then followed by a series of bullets that itemize the points you wish to discuss throughout the meeting. Our favorite bullet is at the bottom and it reads as follows: Is there a fit?

Step 2 – Have No Hidden Agenda

As the prospective client is scanning your agenda, make a powerful statement about your professional code-of-conduct by using a personalized variation of this statement:

"Right up front, I appreciate that you made the time to meet with me today. I know you are a busy person and there are a number of things you could be doing instead of meeting with me and I don't take that lightly. I know you wanted to meet with me to get to know me and my firm and to assess our credentials and competencies and that is what I want to convey in this initial meeting. I wanted to meet with you to determine if we'll have good chemistry over the lifetime of this potential relationship. And because a decision like this is important to both of us, at the end of this meeting, no one has to make any decisions or commitments. We'll both step back and digest what we've discussed. You can take some time to determine if you feel we are a good fit for you. I'll meet with my team and discuss your situation and determine the same. We'll contact you in

48 hours to tell you if we feel we are good fit for each other, is that fair?"

With a personalized version of this approach you will have diffused, disarmed and melted the apprehension away. Think about it. Put yourself in the prospects shoes. What was he expecting based on past experiences?

If you are having a tough time believing in this approach, let us ask you this. After years of dealing with countless consulting clients who have transitioned to this low-key consultative approach, how many times has an entrepreneur called us to say that he contacted a prospect 48 hours later only to be told that he is going with somebody else, or that he's staying with the old provider? It has happened once, and only because the entrepreneur completely reinvented the wheel and as a result, was flawed.

On the other side of the equation, how many entrepreneurs have called us to say that they followed this process but at the end of the meeting the prospective client tried to close the entrepreneur? Countless times. In fact, at a recent seminar we were conducting on this very topic, we were literally interrupted by a client who stood up and informed the crowd, "He's right, this works." Our reply was simple, "This works because it's right. It is professional and it sets the relationship on the right track from the beginning." And keep in mind, how you start a relationship has a profound impact on how it unfolds in the years to come. The tables were turned and the prospective client came to his or her conclusions and was self-motivated. We're not saying it's a universal approach, but we do ask you to determine how it can affect you and customize it accordingly.

So what would you do if the prospective client said, "Look, I'm a busy guy. I don't need to think about it. Everything my buddy said about you has been confirmed in my mind. Plus, I'm going out of town tomorrow. I want to take care of this right now." How would you respond? Would you be consistent and congruent?

We tell our clients to maintain the integrity of the approach by saying this:

"(Name), I appreciate your enthusiasm, I really do. However, this is a process we follow because this is an important decision for both of us. If that is how you feel, I don't think your enthusiasm will fade in 48 hours. Take some time and let me meet with my team. We'll work around your schedule."

That said, in extreme examples there are prospective clients who press you to become clients quite aggressively. You can only deviate from the process under one condition: they are a good fit and perfectly meet your AAA ideal client profile.

For example, let's say the prospect has been referred to you by a great client and at the end of the initial meeting he is relentless about becoming a client. You have to qualify why you deviated:

"I wouldn't ordinarily do this but you are a very good friend of one of our favorite clients and also, you perfectly match our ideal client profile based on AAA. Your desire to take action based on our areas of expertise is perfect. Your attitude is completely consistent with ours and you've demonstrated you think of yourself as an advocate. So, we're prepared to make the exception."

What did we do? We qualified the changed rules of engagement based on an existing client endorsement and the AAA profile. Don't just cave in. It would be like saying, "Okay, it was just a big smoke screen and a test to see if you're serious." You must have integrity, consistency and rules of engagement. Furthermore, you cannot be the only person who gets excited when you do business. You want him to feel just as accomplished, just as good about coming on board with you as you feel about having him come on board. You're looking at fit, you're thinking of the lifetime value of the relationship and he's buying *into* something, he's not buying something. Think of stewardship, not salesmanship. Salesmanship can get you new business, but stewardship is far more attractive. By following this process, you will fast track all new relationships to advocate status and effectively create the desired level of scarcity.

The issue of scarcity does not just apply to prospective clients but rather it is an all encompassing mindset pertaining to your entire clientele. Regardless, the process we just outlined is essential for creating scarcity from the outset of all your client relationships. In developing scarcity, as you continually work to evolve your business, you would do well to adhere to one of the basic and most fundamental laws of business: supply and demand. The *supply* is your availability. Your clients provide the *demand* by requesting your time and services. Your available time is finite. Excess demand creates competition among your clients for your time. By limiting your availability and thus increasing the demand for your time, you are able to differentiate between the clients who *deserve* to see you face-to-face and the ones who *want* to see you.

This discipline results in you spending time with your AAA clients who, as you know, keep you in business. The alternative is to supply too much of your time to those clients who don't contribute very much to the bottom line.

People typically want what they can't have. Look at the world—the things that people place a high value on are those things that are not mass produced nor are they readily available. They are rare—their availability is scarce, not abundant. Seldom do we encounter business owners who even attempt to create scarcity. More often than not, entrepreneurs provide their time to anyone who will listen. Unfortunately, it is the business owner who ultimately pays the price for not limiting his or her access. By applying the scarcity principle, you will attract the clients you want and you will consequently have more time for, what we believe to be most important—time for your family and the pursuit of happiness outside of your business.

Remember

- When meeting with prospective clients, use an agenda and have no hidden agenda.

Take Action Now! (Week 6)

- Use the Sample Agendas and the "Is there a Fit?" scripting contained in the Actionable CD-ROM.

Converting Customers to Fully Empowering Clients

"Gaining all of a client's business stems as much from your philosophy and mindset as it does from your techniques and processes."

– Duncan MacPherson and David Miller

Allow us to ask you this question: Is there a chance, based on the Loyalty Ladder, that you have customers who are not fully aware of everything you do and provide? Chances are the answer is yes, and if so, your MVPs are not just friends and family members of your clients, they are also your existing customers. How do you ask someone to become a client instead of just a customer? How do you communicate your full array of offerings? It begins with your communications about your business being as forthright, clear and precise as possible. All your products and services should be conveyed as a service to your clients, not as something you are trying to sell.

As mentioned, when you first meet with a prospective client they are usually entering into the meeting with some level of apprehension. The prospective client, even one referred to you by an existing client, doesn't necessarily understand exactly what your services and products are. Most business people will immediately focus on what the prospective client has already conveyed to them as their principle interest. For example, an individual may contact a financial advisor about an investment opportunity and not mention that they have a pressing need to re-evaluate their estate planning program.

Being Forthright is Refreshing- to Everyone!

By not introducing yourself properly you miss out on a golden opportunity to set yourself apart from everyone else in your field. You may end up answering their specific questions but leave them wondering about you, your company and the other services you offer.

The process is simple and should be directly referred to in your agenda. Rather than launching into a sales pitch trying to satisfy that immediate need, take a few moments to create rapport and then provide some background information. Tell them a bit about yourself and explain the history and background of your company. Then give them a clear understanding of your approach and show them an outline of your full array of offerings. This can be in a convenient format that can be provided to them for a more careful perusal later. This should only take a few minutes but it sets the prospective client at ease and starts to create a level of trust that other providers typically fail to achieve.

Many entrepreneurs have been trained to ask questions in a first meeting and this is not to be neglected. Remember, it is likely that the person you are meeting with has these questions about you and your company anyway, and you have now conveniently and respectfully provided them with all the answers in an upfront and forthright manner.

Full Disclosure Lights the Path

Once this is completed you can begin to answer the questions necessary to uncover your client's goals and objectives and start determining what it is that you provide that can serve these needs. By disclosing information about yourself first, the prospective client feels comfortable in fully disclosing the information about their situation that you need to make the appropriate decisions. In all likelihood you will have sparked some interest in areas that they would not have revealed to you at this time. The depth of the conversation and level of communication is always enhanced with this approach. The client feels you have their best interest in mind and perceives your full array of offerings as a service that they can take into full consideration and utilize.

To illustrate, the financial advisor we referred to earlier is dealing with a sophisticated array of services and products that requires the ultimate level of trust. We have worked with many financial advisors to create a document called the *Personal Financial Policy Statement.* This document tracks exactly what services have been provided in the past, what the advisor is currently working on with the client and also outlines every service that may become applicable in the future. What it does for the client is it creates clarity and peace of mind. The client gets a copy of the document and can refer to it at anytime.

The format is simple yet precise. An advisor using this tool often finds that the client will initiate conversations about services that the advisor provides but hasn't yet formally introduced. It has been proven on countless occasions to take the abstract or complicated elements of your services down to easy to conceptualize issues for the client. A client never goes to another provider for service that is offered by the advisor and the client often uses the tool as an example to friends and associates to brag about the service that their advisor provides. The *Personal Financial Policy Statement* becomes the centerpiece for all review meetings in the future and a tremendous springboard for promotional partners such as accountants, lawyers, business brokers, etc.

Dealing with people's money is complex on a variety of levels. That said, we're exposed to countless examples where the concept is applicable. One of the consultants in our office recently illustrated the universality of this principle. Our staff member has been engaged in various renovations on his home over the last couple of years. His window supplier made a recommendation to someone who allegedly could be of assistance in designing and building a new foyer to their home. This business person made arrangements to come out and introduce themselves. When they arrived they drove a large truck with the name of a renovation company across it. This immediately sparked some curiosities about their company. The entrepreneur was pleasant enough but dove directly into the problem at hand. He did not tell the prospective client, our staff member, anything about himself, his company, how long they have been in business or anything about the services they offer. After the meeting that was solely focused on this one project, he left to prepare a quote. He robbed himself of the opportunity to create a great first impression and missed out on numerous other opportunities. This was made abundantly clear on his second visit when he started asking things such as who was going to do the tiling and the painting and he was informed that the client had recently secured another subcontractor for that work. By taking just a few moments to talk about himself and his services he would have created an entirely different impression and uncovered thousands of dollars of additional business.

By creating a document for his business that clearly defined his current services and eventually his past deliverables as well as future opportunities, he could have secured a client for the future. You have to keep in mind, people want to know what you do and believe in you, but they've been taught to be disbelieving. This occurs over time because so many people have positioned selling as something you do *to* someone, not *with* or *for* them. Communicate all that you do as a service and it will be interpreted in a much more favorable way. Simplify peoples lives by positioning yourself as a turnkey quarterback.

When you have a professional meeting agenda that promotes full disclosure, new clients will seldom question the agenda or the information you convey. Your planning in such a presentation portrays a benefit to clients from the very beginning of the relationship. Clients are subsequently extremely receptive and accommodating. Most of us, as people, as consumers, would like all the details up front. When we get that information we tend to be accepting and appreciative.

Is It *Too Little, Too Late* to Use Full Disclosure With Existing Customers?

If it is done methodically, professionally, and if it conveys a benefit, you'll be happy to know the full disclosure approach will work like a charm with your existing clientele. Yes, it takes a little longer than with new clients, but it simply proves you should master this approach sooner rather than later. It's easy to forget the majority of your clients do business with you because you're well-liked and respected and not because you've done anything spectacular for them. Your clients like and respect you and are thus quite receptive to a more professional way of doing things, particularly when it is delivered under the umbrella of improved and more professional client service. If you're somewhat apprehensive about how your existing clients will respond, don't worry. The feedback we hear from clients is overwhelmingly appreciative. "It's about time," our clients' clients often say.

We've seen the full spectrum in this area ranging from the very simple to very complex. From a company who does yard maintenance and unveils a "Did You Know?" Campaign explaining their complete array of services including snow clearing and hanging Christmas lights to an accountant who communicates his holistic array of services, the outcomes are the same - if done professionally, converting a partial customer to a fully empowering client can be surprisingly effortless and lead to rapid advocacy.

Making Exceptions - The Slippery Slope

After you have solidified your procedures, it is paramount to avoid making exceptions with respect to gaining a client's complete empowerment. Accepting a customer's transactional business just to make a quick sale can have its consequences. Your code-of-conduct is on display whenever you are in front of prospective clients, but it is also in full gear when those prospective clients leave your office. If you stick to your guns, people will respect you a great deal regardless of whether they do business with you. Eventually, the integrity of consistency gathers steam and you will find it trickling down into all corners of your business. Be faithful to this philosophy and it will come back to reward you in ways you could never have imagined.

If good chemistry exists between you and the prospective client but the prospective client has an aversion to full empowerment because of bad experiences in the past, you may wish to employ this approach:

> *"I appreciate where you are coming from and I feel we are going to have a great relationship. Why don't we do this. I'll take care of your business needs to the extent with which you feel comfort-*

able, now. If, in twelve month's time, I have demonstrated to you my ability to meet those additional needs, I am going to insist you empower me fully. Is that fair?"

This is a bit of a side-bar, but have you ever seen an article in the newspaper announcing some new study or scientific finding which seems too obvious for words? For instance, "Experts say eating too much can make you fat!" It's funny how something so obvious can be positioned as being so profound.

Not long ago we spotted an article with ground-breaking news, "People really appreciate professionalism!" You agree this seems rather obvious too. However, consider all the business owners who simply use a legal pad and pseudo diagnostic approach rather than a prepared agenda and full-disclosure when meeting with new clients. Also, consider the vast number of clients in various market sectors who don't know everything their business providers do. Perhaps the articles were necessary?

To summarize, if a business owner has an effective way of explaining his business and if it's documented into a dedicated Client Process, interesting things start to happen. When clients are taught details about you and your business, meetings become less of an event and more an ongoing process which involves continuous interaction between you and your clients. You effectively teach clients that the relationship will be life long. Documentation of this philosophy, in tandem with written agendas, helps clients to learn all of this more quickly, and it comes across as more professional, too.

Another major benefit of this approach? Your clients can educate others about you in an intelligent and cogent manner. Clients learn to recognize when friends, family members and colleagues are dropping hints about their own business needs and it becomes easy for your clients to spot those who would benefit from your services. This last aspect is enormously important and just one more feature distinguishing your professionalism and thoroughness in separating you from the rest of the pack.

Remember
- Use full disclosure to convey your full array of solutions.

Take Action Now! (Week 7)
- Use the sample Customer to Client Conversion Tool in the Actionable CD-ROM.

Attracting a Higher Quality and Quantity of Referrals

*"The best people to convince others on your behalf are the
people who are already convinced."*

– Marketing Precept

In our seminars and consultations on the topic of referrals, we show entrepreneurs that attracting a higher quality and quantity of referrals from AAA clients stems from using a process rather than using clever phrases or salesmanship.

The first thing we do is explain both the *why* and *how* of referrals. Now you might be saying to yourself, "I don't need to know why, I just want you to explain how!" But here is what we've found. Along the same line of thinking we use for goal setting, when the *why* is clear, the *how* gets much easier to figure out. As we said earlier, the *why* really speaks to purpose and the *how* speaks to process and our experience tells us that purpose is just as important as process.

When we say *why*, we really mean two things. First, why should your clients refer a friend or family member to you? Second, why don't they?

How do you position referrals when you talk to your clients about the concept? Do you position the concept as a service to them or as a favor to you? Most entrepreneurs say things like, "I'm trying to grow my business and I'm always looking for new clients" or something along those lines. In the process they make themselves look needy. You can never bring your needs to your clients. It's not attractive. And keep in mind, it's not what you say that matters but rather what your clients hear when you say something like that. In a moment we will reveal to you our professional and time-tested process that enables you to explain to your clients – new and old – that you will make yourself available as a sounding board for friends and family members who need assistance in your areas of expertise. But remember, you want your clients to feel compelled to introduce a friend to you because it's in their friend's best interest, not yours.

What is Undermining Your Refer-ability?

So have you given any thought to why your clients don't send you referrals? There are several reasons. Perhaps it doesn't occur to them. Perhaps there is an issue of trust. That can mean a lot of things but here is the bottom line, clients are very concerned about how making an endorsement will ultimately reflect back on them. If they're not convinced that you will make them look good, they won't take the risk. Which, as you will see in a moment, is why having a process is so important. When you explain your process it will give your clients clarity to the point that they know exactly what will happen when they steer a friend to you.

Rather than break down all the things that could be undermining your refer-ability, let us propose that you survey your 10 favorite clients with this simple question:

"When you talk about me to a friend, what do you say? How do you describe me?"

Most entrepreneurs who ask their clients this question are shocked by how their clients respond. It's not clear or concise, it's not all-encompassing or accurate and it certainly isn't persuasive. Worst of all though, if your favorite clients can't describe you to you, how can they describe you in an effective manner to a friend when that moment of truth presents itself – that stage of readiness where a friend is ready to listen to your client brag about you.

Our process will essentially enable you to train your clients with the why/who/how. Again, your clients will know *why* they should introduce people - because they will feel they are doing their friends a disservice if they don't. They will know *who* to introduce to you as well. Wouldn't it be great if your clients knew exactly who was a good fit for you based on your areas of expertise? We'll ask you again, have you ever received a referral from a client but you weren't necessarily thrilled with the caliber of the potentially new client? That won't happen again by using our process. And finally, you will be able to show your clients *how* to actually make an introduction by following a process you give them.

The Advocate Referral Process

B elow is a generic variation of our Advocate Process. As you can imagine, we have helped literally hundreds of people customize this approach to suit their own style and needs. There is a slight adjustment you need to make when presenting this process to a new client versus an existing client. New clients have no expectations or frame of reference for how you conduct yourself with respect to referrals. With that in mind, at the signing ceremony when you bring on a new client you can introduce the concept this way:

> *"Mr. Client, as you can see on your agenda, there is a bullet that reads Introducing Friends and Family. I put that there because over the lifetime of my client relationships often a friend or family member will ask about me or a client will feel compelled to make an introduction. Now please understand, I'm not asking you to think of anyone right now, this is simply for down the road."*

By introducing the concept that way, you are hypothetically suggesting that it might happen but not tying it to any expectation. Furthermore, you are not putting them on the spot. This is not a tactic or a form of psychological trickery but the ironic twist to this is that by saying "I'm not asking you to think of anyone right now…" will actually prompt the client to present a name more frequently than when you say, "Can you think of anyone who might need my service? If so, could you give me their name and number."

Continue with:

"Mr. Client, it is important that I explain 'why' I have made the commitment to offer value-added services like this, 'who' is a good fit for my services and then of course, 'how' to get the wheels in motion should a situation present itself."

By doing this you are planting the seed that this is a service and introducing the concept of *why*, *who* and *how*.

"I provide a variety of value-added services that my clients really find to be of value. One of those services includes making myself available to act as a sounding board for friends and family members of my clients who have questions about my type of service. Now please understand, anyone you introduce to me does not need to become a client to take advantage of this service. I will make myself available to offer objective second opinions that your friend can then use to make informed decisions in the future."

This is a powerful component because it tells your client that you aren't being needy nor will you try to sell his friend.

"What is interesting is that on occasion I will meet a friend of a client this way and we really hit it off and we both decide to work together. Let me tell you who those people typically are."

At this point, you simply use your AAA ideal client profile as a tool to take the abstracts of who is a good fit down to something tangible and memorable for your clients. Write AAA on a sheet of paper and break each point down. Explain that you like working with people who take action in areas that are directly suited to your areas of expertise. Describe attitude and advocacy as important elements that you are unwavering on.

> *"I must also say that there are occasions where a client will introduce someone to me who presses me to become a client. However, if I don't feel there would be a good fit based on my AAA profile, I won't bring them on as a client and I hope you'll understand that. I will however introduce them to someone who is a more suitable fit."*

By projecting scarcity you create a cachet in working with you and you give yourself an out if, in fact, you really don't wish to work with someone they refer.

> *"As I've mentioned before, I prefer to think of myself as a specialist rather than a generalist. My goal isn't to see how big I can get, it is to see how small I can stay. I know my capacity and if I go beyond my capacity to serve by trying to be all things to all people, the level of service we provide will get diluted and that will never do. This is why I prefer to be all things to some people and why I stick to that AAA profile."*

This is a powerful validation for your client that they are working with a professional who takes his or her business very seriously. You are making yourself very referable to the right kind of people with this approach.

> *"Now there is a process in place that my clients use for making introductions. If you find yourself in a situation where a friend asks you about me or you feel compelled to recommend me to someone, call me and get the wheels in motion. Tell me about your friend and give me their contact information and we will take it from there. And of course, hold me accountable that anyone you introduce to me will receive the same level of professionalism and confidentiality that you receive."*

Train Your Clients to Reach Out to You

Most people at this point say, "If you find yourself in a situation where you want to make an introduction or somebody asks you about me, give them my card and have them call me." When some entrepreneurs bring on a new client, they hand them a stack of business cards (with the bizarre hope that the client will carry the cards around with them everywhere they go.) without realizing the thickness of the stack of cards has a direct impact on the perception of neediness.

Additionally, you don't know when one of your AAA clients is going to talk about you and your services. But it will happen eventually, and you want your client to be ready. And if your client is talking to a friend and your name or service comes up, if your client says to his friend, "Well, here, call my guy. Here's his phone number. Call him." As easy as it is for his friend to call you, it's easier not to because there's no relationship. Worse than that though is that the Law of Diminishing Intent kicks in. Everyday that goes by that he doesn't call you, the likelihood he ever will fades greatly. Train your clients to come to the rescue.

Let us give you a simple analogy. If we went to a party and we knew all 50 people there but you didn't know anyone, what would be easier for you? If we were to tell you to have fun and mingle? Or would you prefer us to walk around with you, introducing you to people? If you train your clients to tell their friends to call you every time you come up in a conversation, for every ten times that happens, you'll get one call. However, if you train your clients to call on behalf of their friends, nine out of ten times you'll get a call. Your clients already have a relationship with you and are predisposed to advocacy.

As we'll show you in a moment, with existing clients, you need to present this with a slight modification because to them this is new. In the Actionable CD-ROM there is a sample introductory template called The Code-of-Conduct Letter that you can send to your favorite clients to the get the process in play. Or if you choose, the following is an introductory script you can use in an upcoming meeting with an existing client and can be seamlessly integrated with the bulk of the scripting we just provided you above.

> *"Mr. Existing Client, I have recently come to the realization that there are a number of value-added services I provide that many of my clients aren't aware of. I made this realization because recently I asked a number of my clients this simple question: when you talk about me to a friend, how do you describe me? Their answers were all over the map. With that in mind I thought I would quickly explain that one of the value-added services I provide is that I will make myself available to act as a sounding board for friends and family members of my clients."*

You would then go into the rest of the process we described earlier. When you combine this with the service matrix, AAA client profiling, organization and structure as well as a procedures manual, you have made yourself extremely referable.

If you take the high-road and if you are understated, referrals can really be positioned as a service. You are essentially explaining the fulfillment that comes from helping people make informed decisions. Successful decision-making is a matter of choice, not chance. Your sense of purpose in terms of *why* you are in business is tied to helping people make informed decisions, whether or not these people are or ever become clients. If you can convey that, you will attract a steady stream of quality endorsements.

Referral Checklist

1. **Ensure Your Phraseology is Attractive**

   Many business owners tend to over-use the word *referral* in their client communications. While the word is not inherently bad, we believe it tends to make one appear needy, speaking more about how you benefit, rather than how the client benefits. We urge you to incorporate the words *introduce* and *recommend* when you communicate the referral concept to your clients. This speaks more to an activity than it does to your productivity.

2. ***Commoditize* the Referral Process.**

   Our research shows it is not uncommon for a business owner's clients to feel a little handcuffed when talking about the business provider – *you* – in an intelligent fashion. Help them sound more compelling or they will develop their own phraseology (and you might not like what they choose to say). Tell them exactly how to refer you and make this a dedicated part of your business. This is why the AAA concept is so helpful.

   It might sound foreign or make you uncomfortable at first, but it's crucial to script your recommendation message, rehearse it, then teach your clients to relay it when an opportune moment arises. A wishy-washy approach leads to wishy-washy results. You may get referrals from a casual approach, but if you want predictable results, use a consistent and dedicated approach.

Capture and chronicle your approaches. Show your team how it's done and have them follow suit. With easy-to-follow, predictable procedures come predictable successes.

3. **Launch The Code-of-Conduct Letter to Existing Clients**

If you are reluctant to spring your new and improved advocate process on existing clients in person, you can send out a personalized version of this letter to open the door in a low-key manner. This simple letter can be mailed by itself, included within a newsletter, with an invoice or as a dedicated piece in your review or update kit. In a nutshell, it describes for your client what occurs when you meet with the person your client recommended. This approach facilitates the recommendation process for your clients, helping them to conceptualize it and relay it to their friends. It also builds confidence in your clients and as a result they know you take this issue seriously and you'll make them look good when they recommend you.

Dear ... (personalized),
As you know, one of the most fulfilling aspects of my job is in helping people make informed decisions about their business needs. The puzzle has many pieces, and I truly enjoy helping people put those pieces together. In this way, I can help my clients face the future with anticipation, not apprehension, and this is especially important during times of economic uncertainty.

What's more, one of my biggest responsibilities is to help people referred to me by my clients. When someone endorses me to a friend or family member, they are putting their name on the line, and I don't take that lightly. I owe it to my clients to do a good job.

So if you feel compelled to introduce me to a friend, give me a call and get the wheels in motion. Your friend does not need to become a client to gain access to me and I will act as a sounding board to help him or her make informed decisions in the future.

4. Imprint Everywhere

Once you've introduced your referral process to your clients, you can't expect that they will remember it over the lifetime of your relationship, keep reminding them. Trigger that moment of familiarity and recognition every chance you get. And here's what's great. In virtually every form of communication you have with your clients you can be reminding them subtly and professionally about the concept of referrals – in phone calls, newsletters, review meetings, letters, every form of communication. Every time you talk to a client you have the chance to remind them about the concept of referrals in a very high-road manner. Take the call rotation as an example. Your client has been with you for six months. He's in your call rotation. In your conversation you ask him, "Hey, how's it going?" What you're looking for in this conversation is an opportunity for him to open the door so you can say something. You ask, "How's business?" He says, "Fantastic. How's yours?" The door is open for you to respond by saying, "It's funny you should ask because recently a couple of my clients have introduced a friend or family member who's been interested in what we do or simply looking for the reassurance of a second opinion. You remember the process if that happens, right? Just give us a call. I don't want to claim miracles, but I'll either validate the track they're on is right, or reveal a few minor adjustments they could make. Minor adjustments could lead to major improvements down the road but either way, if they're a friend of yours, I'll make the time to answer their questions. And of course they don't need to become a client. I'll simply make myself available."

PS – Letters to Clients are Great For Referral Reminders

The PS at the bottom of your letters is the most vividly read part of your correspondence and is a great place to put a call-to-action for referrals. As you know, a call-to-action is simply when you tell someone what you want them to do.

We love calls-to-action. A shampoo company increased their sales by 30% with one call to action? They put the call-to-action on the directions of the shampoo. (It's weird they need directions on how to use shampoo!) What was their call-to-action? The directions said, "put in, rinse out." Or words to that effect. What was the call-to-action? "Repeat." Sales went up 30%, consumption went up 30%. Next time you get a referral from a client, just say to them, repeat. (You never know – kidding!)

> *PS. Now would be a great time to thank my clients for recommending me to their friends and family throughout the year. As you know, my business has been built on word-of-mouth advertising, and I take it as a tremendous compliment that you have the confidence in me to wave my flag. It really means a lot. I treat it as a huge responsibility and one that I never take lightly. Thanks.*

You're not asking for a referral, you're simply reminding clients about the concept.

Again, it comes down to what is called stage-of-readiness. You don't know when a client will have the opportunity to talk about you to someone within their inner circle, but the opportunity will present itself. You want your client to be ready to persuasively describe you and then act as the bridge.

What are your clients saying now to their friends when the moment-of-truth occurs? What do you want your client to do? Do you want them to give their friends your number with a simple, "You gotta call my guy, he's great"? Or would you prefer they ask if they should call on their behalf? Your clients should be saying, "As a value-added service, my guy makes himself available and you don't even need to become a client." Does any of this happen by chance, or by choice? It is by design. We don't mean to oversimplify this but conveying the *why*, *who* and *how* is time-tested and proven to work. When positioned as a service it's not only effective but it will feel right to you.

Frame Your Way to Success

This concept, although simple, has repeatedly proven effective. Frame the following quote in a simple 8" x 10" frame and hang it on the wall in your office. Or put it on the back of your business card.

"A referral is a huge responsibility. It is also the highest compliment a client can give you and should never be taken lightly."

– Anonymous

If we had had a nickel for every instance one of our clients told us of clients who, upon seeing the framed quote, said "I didn't know you were accepting new referrals," or, "I thought you were too busy to accept new clients," or, "It never occurred to me to refer a friend to you," well, we'd be writing this book from a villa in Tuscany.

Before we move on, another gentle reminder about implementation. We encounter an extraordinary number of business owners who enroll in our Coaching and Consulting program who are – unbeknownst to them - on the verge of a breakthrough in their business.

Typically, over the course of their careers, business owners experience dramatic growth in terms of expertise and sophistication. However, the systems in the business do not get developed at the same rate. The resulting disparity can be frustrating. The business owner hears about terrific activities like the Client Advisory Council, Advocate Process, etc. – yet nothing gets implemented. No matter how cognizant they are of a great idea, they simply do not have the infrastructure to implement it and translate it into results. Referrals are far too important to take lightly, so here is quick summary checklist to inspire you implement the Advocate Process, if nothing else:

- Do clients know what they can expect from me when I meet a friend of theirs?
- Do they know my ideal client profile?
- Do they have a clear representation of my approach to service and could they tell others about it?
- How can I keep them informed and up-to-date regularly and consistently?
- Do they know the processes and steps of how to introduce someone to my services?
- What are these steps exactly?
- Do clients know how I am paid?
- Are they familiar with my team, and the responsibilities of each individual?

If your clients don't know the answers to these questions, ask yourself, "Why not?" If you are confident you have done a good job at educating your clients, have you documented your procedures?

Would your job be easier if your clients were eminently capable of answering each of these questions in detail? Would be easier for them to refer you to others? In our experience, the answer is a resounding, "Yes!"

Remember

- You don't need to ask for referrals. Position referrals as a service to your clients rather than as a favor to you and then remind them that you accept them throughout the lifetime of your relationship.

Take Action Now! (Weeks 8 & 9)

- Customize and then gain mastery of The Advocate Process in the Actionable CD-ROM and begin the process of introducing it to your clients.

Reciprocate

Create Promotional Partnerships and Strategic Alliances

"If you want people to buy into your goals and dreams,
start by buying into theirs."

– Duncan MacPherson and David Miller

The R in DART stands for Reciprocity. This is a crucial part of your activity plan because if you think about the Law of Reciprocity, giving really starts the receiving process.

If you look back on the concept of building pillars to create multiple income streams, once you have your client pillar chugging along your second pillar should be that of promotional partners. These are other like-minded professionals in your marketplace who are interested in collaborating with someone like you. When you think of the concept of MVP's, the clients of these partners are some of your most predisposed prospects.

The key with promotional partnering is that it has to be, as with our entire philosophy, positioned as a service. Many entrepreneurs attempt to engage in various forms of collaboration and the process unravels because they telegraph their motivation as simply a money grab. Yes, your approach must be forthright and transparent but the philosophy behind it must be clear - you are trying to simplify peoples lives and deliver value-added services that they'll actually value.

We've been exposed to countless examples of promotional partnering from a variety of sectors in the marketplace. We've seen accountants collaborate with lawyers and financial advisors for estate planning luncheons, (if only their names were Rice, Currie and Lamb). We heard a story about a veterinarian who created a strategic alliance with a taxidermist (their slogan could be, "Either Way, You'll Get Your Dog Back!"). While some examples are more sophisticated than those, this is still one of our favorites. We were in Tampa a while back and got into a cab from the airport to the hotel convention center where the conference we were attending was being held. The cab driver was a nice guy and asked where we were from. We told him, "Canada." And we all started talking about hockey. Big surprise. We had a great chat. (He didn't know where Calgary or Kelowna was, but he laughed hysterically when we told him that Calgary was so flat you could watch your dog run away for three days!)

Anyway, when he asked what kind of work we did, we told him, "Marketing and business consultants." He said, "I love marketing. Want to hear a great story?" He starts to tell us about this restaurant in Tampa called Burns Steakhouse. We'd never been there, but apparently it's legendary. "Here's what's cool about Burns. They're really good. But," he said, "as a cab driver, if I drop somebody off at

Burns for dinner, after I drop them off, I get to drive around back and I get a free steak." That's pretty powerful. Think about it. Somebody gets into his cab, or any cab, and says I'm hungry take me somewhere, where are we going? I can just see him salivating, "Oh we've gotta go to Burns. I mean, *you've* gotta go to Burns." This guy is an influencer. He says Burns is so good, they could survive just on word-of-mouth from their clients, but they thrive because of the endorsements from these very powerful influencers.

A Great and Supportive CAST

You too could be a powerbroker and create a community of collaborative professionals, but where do you start? Well, as usual, a great jumping off point would be to look at your favorite clients. We have an acronym – big surprise – CAST. **Client Advisory Support Team** You can actually create a formalized network of the people with whom you collaborate.

We arrived at the acronym CAST in an attempt add some personality to the concept and make it memorable. If you really get into the spirit of the concept you'll see that it can unfold like the production of a stage play.

In our analogy, clients are the audience. The script is written for their critical eye. The person making the recommendations and planning for the best possible outcome in the business provider-client relationship is you, the *director*. The business system - your duplicable interaction with clients - serves as the *script* and it is a well thought-out plan of action. Finally, the business professionals who help to implement the plan are the *actors*.

Think of your best client. Who is his director with respect to the services and products he needs? In keeping with our dramatic production analogy, as the director of a production you should be in direct contact with the actors to actively implement the script.

The greatest threat to a director occurs when a client gives another director the opportunity to look at the script.

> **Q:**   How does this happen?
>
> **A:**   It would be easy to say clients allow this to happen because they don't have a relationship with their director based on an inherent level of trust. The opposite is true. Directors allow this to happen because they haven't made the effort to build trust-based relationships with their clients. It's that simple.

> **Q:**   How do other directors make contact with another director's client?
>
> **A:**   Affluent people talk to other affluent people. *Source One* for this type of contact is the personal recommendation of a family member or friend.

Source Two is, more importantly, the professional recommendation. Let's say, in this scenario, an accountant is recommending a financial advisor to his client. The client is very open to this type of professional recommendation because of the existing trust-based relationship with the professional making the recommendation.

However, as the director of the financial script, if you're the financial advisor, this type of incident is less likely to occur because you are integral in implementing the plan. You become the common factor linking the financial professionals involved in implementing a financial plan and the client.

Q: Should I recommend other business providers to a client? Why would I want to go to that trouble?

A: Yes, you should. It is easier than you think to recommend clients to CAST members you know and trust. After all, you should be developing open lines of communication with a client regarding all matters pertinent to their business. Recommending professionals who do excellent and necessary work is your responsibility, particularly if you're interested in your client's business remaining not only afloat, but also viable and ultimately successful.

The positive results are threefold. First, the client is more likely to remain loyal to you as a source of good information, thus reducing the chances they will be recommended away from you. Secondly, you secure your position as the primary relationship. Last but not least, creating a solid, reliable and trustworthy CAST will benefit the client immensely and will encourage the client to recommend other affluent people who seek this type of comprehensive service.

Director's Notes

Keep in mind these basic and important facts about affluent clients.

1. Affluent clients use a wide array of solutions. Do you know who those professionals are? They should be recommended and directed by you and/or be aware of your relationship with the client.

2. In the majority of cases a client is recommended to a CAST member by a friend, family member, associate or another member of the client's CAST. You should make every effort to be the person directing the recommendations. Your relationship with the client should be the primary relationship within the CAST network.

3. Usually a client's CAST members work in isolation. This is an opportunity for a proactive director to take the leading role in the CAST by integrating the members of the CAST and ensuring all are reading the same script.

4. Each member of the CAST has a unique ability which adds strength to the overall production.

5. Like the director, other CAST members encourage and welcome recommendations and introductions to prospective clients.

6. In most cases, a client will have a lawyer, accountant, tax preparer, banker or insurance agent they are using or have used in the past. However, it does not follow that they are satisfied with the services provided by these professionals. Do not make assumptions. Ask the important questions. You may be surprised by the answers.

An effective CAST campaign may be implemented in the following steps.

Step #1
Begin developing a group of professionals for your best clients. You need look no further than your best clients. Poll each client for the members of **their** Client Advisory Support Team. You are, in essence, building a community and network of like minded, non-competitive business professionals who need each other's services. (You could conduct a CAST Advisory Council to support this as it gathers momentum.) Every name represents the potential for a professional relationship. Contact each of these professionals and arrange an introductory meeting with the purpose of mutual aware-

ness about the client you have in common. If, during this meeting, you are impressed by the services offered, consider recommending the person as a member of the CAST you offer to other clients. Like you, all CAST professionals prefer to work by recommendation and they will welcome the opportunity to play a role in your business.

Step #2

The second objective is to find a CAST member with whom your client is unhappy. This is a golden opportunity to replace this person with a member from your list of CAST members. By doing this, you are consolidating your position in the primary relationship.

Step #3

The third objective is to build high-trust relationships with CAST members and potential CAST members. Most business owners have experienced the situation where they've provided multiple referrals to an accountant or lawyer, for instance, only to be forgotten at subsequent client meetings. Such situations occur because referrals are not sufficient incentive for people to reciprocate. A referral is really only a type of lead.

A recommendation, on the other hand, is very different. It assumes a transfer of trust from one professional to another. As we've mentioned on several occasions, the most crucial elements of a professional career are trust and integrity. Most professionals will not risk losing these elements with a client by making light of a recommendation made to another professional. In other words, you must develop a high degree of trust with CAST members.

In order to build high levels of trust, you must demonstrate consistency, congruency, credibility and, above all, integrity and accountability. The rule of relationship building is to be patient, as it will take time, and to have frequent contact based on genuine intent.

In the beginning stages of a professional relationship, merely referring business will not build the level of trust you need in order to create a successful CAST. Referring business is a given. Beyond that, you must construct a deliberate, meaningful service package for your CAST members and potential CAST members, one that you deliver consistently.

In this way, a CAST member is much like a client. Some examples you may wish to use in your CAST package are quarterly phone calls, articles of interest, invitations to select client events, copies of your newsletter and annual anchors (such as Thanksgiving/birthday cards). Once you have decided on your approach, enter it into your contact management system to ensure consistency. As recommendations start to come back to you, send acknowledgment for the trust and confidence, rather than for the business itself. A note such as, *"Thank you for the continued trust and confidence."* instead of *"Thank you for the business."* should be used.

It is Worth the Effort

Creating, directing and supporting a CAST is not an easy task. It is similar to developing a solid base of affluent clients through the process of building client confidence and encouraging client recommendations. You may ask yourself, "Is this degree of effort going to be worth it? I have spent considerable time and effort building my client base. Why bother with a CAST when I can enjoy the benefits of my existing client base?" Unless you are completely confident you are indispensable and irreplaceable to each and every affluent client, you need to secure the relationship you have with your clients. Being the director of a trusted, competent CAST will build a virtual wall around your clients. The value of your relationship with your clients will increase exponentially as you secure your position as the director of their business provisions.

You might be interested in knowing, to bring it all together, we know people who have taken the following and put it onto a plastic bookmark and sent it to their clients.

"You know, I'm very well connected in the business community and I have clients calling me all the time asking me if I know someone in a specific area of business and if I can make an introduction. Here is a listing of the various companies with whom we have very good relationships. Just slide this into your yellow pages and if ever you need any of these (i.e. accountant, computer guru,

etc.) call me and I'll make an introduction."

They've become power brokers. Your clients will call and say, "Well, I want to buy a new car. Should I buy or lease?" Even if you're not in the car business, you can say, "Let me make a call for you." Become the rainmaker. You look out for people, they look out for you. The Law of Reciprocity. It's powerful. Be sure to explain the rules of engagement to anybody you recommend. Simply say,

"Look. If I ever introduce somebody to you, the world stops. You drop everything and you just absolutely shower this person in goodwill and service. And I'll do the same."

Before we shift gears, we'll say it again, your best prospective clients are the friends and family members of your existing clients. They are number one. Your second best are existing customers, who could become clients. A close third on the MVP list are the clients of promotional partners.

Remember
- Be a Power Broker. Giving really does start the receiving process.

Take Action Now! (Week 10)
- Review the CAST scripting and process in the Actionable CD-ROM.

Thank

"Not saying thanks when a client brings value to you would be like not feeding the goose that lays the golden eggs."

– Marketing Maxim

The *T* in DART is for Thanks. New clients, existing clients, promotional partners, vendors and staff bring value to you every day. A major part of your code-of-conduct must include activities that demonstrate and pay tribute to that value. In a perfect world, these moments of truth would never go unrecognized.

When Someone Becomes a New Client

It is a big deal when new clients empower you to provide products or services, especially if they have left another business provider. Remember, it's all about contrast. They are obviously leaving their former provider for a reason. Once they move over to you, they are going to compare the two of you. Furthermore, if that client has been referred to you by a client or strategic alliance, you know those two people – the referrer and the new client - are eventually going to meet and talk about you. What do you do to ensure the new client not only makes favorable comparisons in his own mind, but also goes back to the source of the referral and describes how he was dazzled? Your efforts will go a long way towards prompting your new client to say, "You were right. She really is great!"

At the very least, you must send a personalized thank-you card immediately after bringing on a new client. Mere moments after the proverbial signing ceremony, send a nice card which will have impact and shelf life. Please be careful with the phraseology. Do not write, "Thanks for the business." This only recognizes the benefits to you. Make the message about them. Write something which demonstrates to the client you were really paying attention. Make reference to something they revealed to you about themselves.
For example:

> *"I really enjoyed meeting with you today. It was fun listening to you talk about your new boat. I'm looking forward to a great relationship. Welcome aboard!"*

The bottom line is for you to be understated yet radiate an attractive impression. You don't actually need the business. You'll take it, but you don't need it. By conveying to new clients your utmost fulfillment comes from meeting and working with great people, you make a powerful statement about your commitment to helping people achieve their goals.

The thank-you card is just the start. We've seen business owners use a sequence of a four or five step process following the card. These other steps, implemented during the first 30 to 45 days of the new relationship, are designed to counter any buyers remorse and further validate the client's decision to select you while fast-tracking him or her to advocate status.

The New Client Welcome Process

In order to provide yourself the infrastructure necessary to best handle all the new business you'll be generating and enable the acquisition of even more new business, take a good look at your New Client Welcome Process. Although this is just one small component of the many we're discussing and advocating, it is an important component and one you can easily implement. We recommend this five-step process (or something similar) for two simple reasons. In addition to the conversation your new client will inevitably have with the person who introduced the two of you, a new client who has been referred is predisposed to referring someone else as well. Why? They have – themselves - just been through the process and were (ideally) dazzled. They are better qualified than anyone else to refer you. This is especially true at the beginning of your relationship when their enthusiasm for you is fresh. People like to brag. Give them something to brag about.

When we work with our consulting clients, we spend a considerable amount of time and thought on this aspect of their client relationships. Here is an abridged version of the *New Client Welcome Process* which you can implement with minimal expense.

Step 1

Start archiving FORM (Family, Occupation, Recreation, Message) information on the client and family from beginning

116

of your relationship with every client. If they ever ask why you need non-business specific information, use the following to help explain your intentions in a positive way. *"It is one of my top goals to bring my clients exceptional value, and it helps me to do a better job if I know what it is they value."*

Step 2

As mentioned, be sure to send a nice card after the initial meeting to continue the chemistry-building process. Personalize your greeting and write it by hand. Try to include something the two of you discussed.

Step 3

Approximately one week after the new client has come on board, send a formal welcome letter informing the client of your appreciation at being selected. Also mention that you and your team understand the scope of responsibility involved. Introduce the members of your team, including their job descriptions and telephone numbers. Add a PS to remind your new client that you and your team are always available to answer questions for friends and family members, too.

Step 4

Approximately two weeks after the new client has come on board, send a nice-quality welcome binder complete with divider tabs and a letter. In the letter, explain your realization of the vast quantities of information we all receive and your pride in helping people stay organized. The tabs could be labeled according to the services you provide. Also be sure to include your Full Listing of Services document. They will refer to this as their needs change in the future. Drop it off yourself if you have time.

Step 5

When your new client receives their first statement or invoice from your firm, have a team member call to walk them through it and answer any questions or concerns they may have. This refreshingly courteous call is part of the contrast-building process designed to demonstrate your code-of-conduct. If you follow this process, your new clients will feel as though they have received more value from you in the first few days than they did from their former provider in an entire year. As a result, you are much more referable.

Saying Thanks for a Referral - Feed the Goose

An endorsement is one of the biggest compliments - and responsibilities - you receive. Show your clients you don't take the vote of confidence lightly. Pay tribute to the activity, not the productivity. Rather than sending a card saying, "Thanks for referring Bob to me," say instead, "Thanks for introducing Bob to me." Again, this slight adjustment in phraseology does not speak to your needs.

We'll say it again, you can never look needy. The marketplace rewards what we earn and deserve. A profound distinction exists between seeming demanding or needy and being deserving. When you take the latter – the high road – people will be easily convinced to work with you and will go to work convincing other people on your behalf. A word of caution. As the referral floodgates slowly begin to swing open, don't take them for granted by letting an *entitlement* mindset creep in. Say *thanks* in a meaningful way that has *both impact and shelf life* and the river will continue to flow. Here is an example that was a near-miss but close to the mark and it illustrates the point of paying tribute:

We have a friend in the leasing business. We sent him a huge referral. Huge! It made his year. He knows we play golf, so he sent a few sleeves of golf balls. We called him laughing to say, "Hey, nice impact, lousy shelf life." The balls didn't last long. A while later we talked to him about a subscription to a golfing magazine. About the same cost, same impact. What's the shelf life? Every month for a year, whenever that magazine arrives, we'd be thinking about him.

Again, the best way to have impact is to apply FORM, as was the case in this example:

We know one business owner whose client's son was a sports nut and loved hockey. After this particular client sent a meaty referral to our client, our client responded by sending the father and son a pair of hockey tickets. Pretty good, we thought. Our client didn't stop there. He also dug deep and sent the son an NHL jersey! Now that was effective, and certainly more enduring than candy. Every time the son wears the jersey, what goes through his Dad's mind?

Good Branding is Outstanding

An essential component that ties the Advocate Referral Process together with Saying Thanks to your clients for the value you bring, is to create personal branding that people can identify with. Good branding personifies and differentiates you. Your brand is what makes you different, outstanding and enables your clients to easily see why and how you and your services are special. Thus, your clients can easily wave your flag with meaningful specifics. Without these specifics, you run the danger of swimming in a pool of sameness where, rather than being indispensable to your clients, you are interchangeable with your competitors.

Establish a Foundation

Cicero, in ancient Rome said, "Ask not what your community can do for you, ask what you can do for your community." We all know the more popularized version of that quote but the spirit has a direct correlation to entrepreneurs. By that we mean, inject a community feel into your marketing efforts to say *thanks* for everything you get from it and also to help establish your personal brand.

Identify with a community event or charitable organization or create one of your own. Sponsor a rising sports star. Create a scholarship for kids that you will contribute to every time you bring on a new client or receive a referral. Not only does it contribute to your business success and brand identity, it also contributes to your personal fulfillment.

Milestone Recognition

On a frequent basis, a meaningful event, or milestone, occurs in your clients' lives. This is a moment-of-truth that you could pay tribute to.

We have a financial advisor client who, in a conversation with *his* best client said, "So, what are you doing this weekend?" His best client answered, "Oh, we're going to my son's graduation." The best client continued with details of his long-time concerns the kid would never get through school, it took a long time, stops and starts, trips to Europe, the kid had to *find himself* and so on. Our client tells us about the conversation and our first response was, "That's soul baring. That's not something everybody would do, it says a lot about your relationship. This guy trusts you. What are you going to do? This Moment-of-Truth could take your relationship to another level all together." Our client didn't have an answer, so we gave him one. "Go out and buy the book, The Richest Man in Babylon."

Our client sent the book to the kid with a card congratulating him. The kid of a number one client (Again, remember the advice of Confucius, "Dig your well before you're thirsty."). The card said, "Hey, congratulations. Way to go! This is the only book you'll need to ensure your financial future." And the kid's father - the best client - called back and said, "That was impressive, my son read it in one sitting. If I would have given it to him, he wouldn't have read it. It came from you and transformed the way he thinks about money. You should hear him."

Improving Communication is Key

You already know, but here's a gentle reminder. The single activity which has the greatest impact on your ability to competitor-proof your favorite clients and stimulate quality referrals is consistent communication. Proactively convey to a client you genuinely value the relationship. This is without question the foundation of your daily marketing code-of-conduct. Clearly, the cornerstone of this message is the style and manner in which you demonstrate your sincere appreciation when the client brings value to you.

There are all kinds of **moments-of-truth** examples that you could be responding to. (We discussed a number of them back when we talked about FORM.) A client has a meaningful birthday or anniversary. Pay tribute to these things. They're important. Another client expands his business and moves to a new, larger facility. Have a professional photographer to take a picture of their new building. Get it framed. It won't cost a lot of money but the impact and shelf life are huge. Stop for a second, pay tribute, say thanks when these moments-of-truth occur. Make an effort to stand out.

Remember

- When someone brings value to you, that is a moment-of-truth that defines your relationship. Pay tribute in a way that has impact and shelf life.

Take Action Now! *(Week 11)*

- Refer to the Milestone and Moment-of-Truth guidelines in the Actionable CD-ROM and strive to make this process habitual.

A Final Word Before We Shift From Client-Centered Marketing to Prospecting

As we alluded to earlier, the key to success is to make the implementation of DART-related activities habitual. The best way to achieve that is to create automated processes that you and your team can deploy effortlessly. They are the surefire way to create consistency in your business. As you know, your clients crave consistency because it is the foundation of trust in all levels of the business world. People use a drive-thru repeatedly not because of the quality of the food but because it saves time and they know what to expect. They trust it. People stay loyal to a dentist because expectations will at least be met, if not, exceeded. The moment the service falls below expectations, cracks in the loyalty foundation begin to appear.

At the risk of getting too technical, an automated process is defined as any repetitive activity involving a series of different steps. Customer service is an excellent example. Set up your database to remind you of activities relative to clients' FORM information. Depending on the classification of each client, you and your team may have up to 25 activities or "touches" per year for a AAA client. For instance, by coding your clients in the database and then by designing your service matrix – that is the specific activities for each client classification – the database will automatically notify you or the appropriate member of your team when any of these activities are to be completed. These activities can then be set up to renew on an annual basis for an indefinite period of time. To qualify as an *automated process*, we look for an activity requiring multiple steps to be sequentially completed. Therefore, anything in your business system meeting this criterion can have an automated process designed for it. New Client Welcome, Anniversary or Milestone Recognition or anything else which comes to mind can be included. As always, your FORM information will prove to be invaluable.

Identify, recognize and define automated processes. It's important. Automated processes promote consistency, congruency, understanding and they create expectations. Clients learn your patterns and come to expect them. Once the expectations have been set, and met, your clients will communicate your patterns to others. When they do, people like themselves are naturally and easily recommended to you.

To create one automated process, you must create an architecture which can be converted to a digital format. The digital format is then housed on your database. As a result, you will not have to be concerned with the ensuing steps on a daily basis. The database informs each and every person in your organization exactly what is to be completed and when.

Four steps are involved in creating an automated process.
1. Name the process and provide a short description for others to understand the purpose.
2. Record each step of the process.

3. Define the specific elements of each step. The elements are *who, what, when* and *how.*

4. Store all this information in the database. The database will monitor and ensure activity as well as ensuring completion.

Once your automated processes are in place you, your staff, and your clients will notice a significant difference in how you interact.

Shameless Plug For Our 8020Platform

Clearly the concept of automated processes inspired us to create the 8020Platform. If you aren't interested in reinventing the wheel, visit our website at www.8020platform.com and allow us to shine the light on the platform. This will enable you to determine if it is a fit for your business.

Prospect Target Marketing

Once you have your client pillar predictably producing revenue you can then extend to promotional partnering pillar. If, after deploying and refining the processes for the first two and you still find yourself with excess time capacity, then, and only then, can you consider the third pillar – Prospect Target Marketing.

Don't misinterpret what we're saying here, prospecting can be an integral part of your business development approach and mindset. Our concern however – and this stems from witnessing countless examples first-hand – is that we don't want you to pursue prospect target marketing at the expense of lower hanging fruit.

Let's come full circle to the MVP concept. Your Most Valuable Prospects are as follows:

- Friends and Family Members of existing clients based on the Rule of 52;
- Customers who could become fully empowering clients based on the Loyalty Ladder;
- Clients of promotional partners based on the Law of Reciprocity and CAST; and/or
- Target Market Prospects.

Based on the above list, be certain that you have the first 3 opportunities predictably and sustainably chugging along before you engage in pure target market prospecting.

Some would dispute this approach saying that they don't have time to wait for their first two pillars to start baring additional fruit. Prospecting can garner more immediate impact. If you are thinking that way, consider this, we have clients that haven't engaged in pure prospecting in years. Zero. They have adopted the "attract rather than chase" mindset and philosophy and view every expenditure of effort with clients as an investment that will always pay the best return.

That said, if you are new to business and don't have a lot of existing clients yet or if you have the first two pillars humming along you can then certainly consider these concepts sooner – however stay true to the code-of-conduct philosophy for your clients even if the numbers are currently small. It's still the best way to make the numbers big.

On to Prospecting

Let's differentiate between advertising and prospective target marketing. We're not the biggest fans of classic advertising for small entrepreneurs for a variety of reasons. First, there is an old saying, "Half of all advertising is wasted. We just don't know which half." A lot of advertising is spray and pray. Throw stuff out there and hope for the best. Results of promotional efforts must be quantifiable. Don't engage in *hope* advertising, where you just hope it's going to work. Just because your competitors are doing it or just because you have the budget, doesn't mean it is appropriate for you.

Prospect Target Marketing is an entirely different conversation. It is far more precise and efficient. Advertising is broadcasting, target marketing is narrowcasting. It might not be as glamorous but the return on investment is dramatically better.

Avoid Spray and Pray Marketing

We know what were talking about here. Every now and again we get lured back into the black hole known as broadcasting. When we started promoting our 8020Platform, we bought full page ads in magazines that, while being targeted to our audience, was classic spray and pray. We'd talk about the attributes of our Platform and create compelling reasons why readers should visit our website and take the tour. We got faked out because the magazine had a circulation of 80,000 readers. We thought, "how could we go wrong?" When the dust cleared, 100 people would go to our website and a couple would buy.

Advertising is interruptive, broadcast marketing is interruptive. You're flipping through a magazine, you stop, it's interrupting what you're doing. We're hoping you'll take action. We're going out looking for a buyer and hope that we stumble into one.

Our point in mentioning this right up front is simple. We want you to scrutinize your current prospecting efforts and ask yourself if they are quantifiably impactful or if they are broadcast hope marketing approaches.

There are so many different prospecting options. Contrast the inter-ruptive magazine campaign we just described to our next effort. We then launched our search engine optimization campaign and adwords campaign on Google. (There are a variety of good books on the topic available.)

This campaign was so much more effective first and foremost because we turned the tables. With the broadcasting campaign, we hoped people would stumble into our ad, stop what they were doing and visit our website. With the search engine campaign and adwords click search campaign, people came looking for us. When people searched on Google for the trigger words we selected, our ads came up on the side. People who were predisposed clicked on them and instantly went to our website. In our initial test campaign, we spent $1800 and received in excess of 900 hits to our website. Keep in mind, these were people who were looking for what we sold, we weren't looking for them. (It was far more effective, but still not as effective as our Tell-A-Friend referral campaign – just a reminder about the importance of client marketing.)

Broadcasting is expensive, it's time-consuming, it's laborious and worst of all it sets you up for the most brutal emotion in marketing – *Antic-appointment!* You put it out there, you cross your fingers, anticipate, but are – in the end – disappointed. Trade shows, bill-boards, radio, newspaper ads, cold-calling and the like are broad-casting efforts that are often the least efficient yet most expensive ways to prospect. They can give a certain measure of instant gratifi-cation, but after that it's like a shooting star, fading quickly and for-gotten. (We worked a trade show booth a long time ago that was a complete waste of time – on a hourly basis we earned less money than a parking meter.)

Narrowcasted marketing is the way to go. You zero-in on specific, high-value, geographic, demographic, socio-economic target markets and turn them upside down methodically over a period of time.

Specialize, Don't Generalize

The first point to consider on narrowcasting is this, position yourself as a specialist. There are two types or marketers, spe-cialists and generalists. As we've said before, generalists try to be all things to all people. Specialists try to be all things to some people and in the process radiate more cachet and professionalism.

The key point of difference is that specialists are patient. The first thing they do once they've identified a target market is they develop an insiders reputation. This is achieved when the prospects within your target market identify you as being elite and head and shoulders above your competitors. One of the best ways to achieve this is to identify an inside champion who can help you understand your target market better and in the process make yourself more attractive.

As usual, the best place to start is with your clients. Think about your clients. Who are your favorites? What do they do? Where do they live? Choose one. We had this same conversation with another of our clients – a very bright and successful financial advisor. As we discussed this concept with him, he revealed that his number one client owned an engineering firm. We said, "Engineers. Let's target engineers." He said, "Nope. I don't want another engineer." (Apparently he had some issues with engineers!) His second best client was a dairy farmer (referred to him by his assistant's dad, who happened to be a dairy farmer). We asked, "How's your relationship with this guy?" "Uh, fantastic," he told us. We advised, "Take him out for lunch, pick his brain and basically ask him what you need to do to make yourself attractive to people just like him." Tell him, "If I had my way, I'd have 100 clients like you. You perfectly match my profile, and I just love being around you." Our client called us after that little lunch and said, "This is going to be amazing. He told me everything to do, where I need to go." Our advice? "Develop an insider's reputation where other dairy farmers view you as a specialist." Do you know there is a magazine called Holstein Journal? Everything you ever wanted to know about cows. Enough stuff to talk about cows to fill a magazine every month. Not only did he read the magazine, he actually had some of his articles published in it. You walk into his office today and you'll see pictures of his clients standing beside their big cows with ribbons on them. He became the go-to guy for dairy farmers. Instead of being all over the map, he narrowed his focus, became a specialist, increased his visibility, built an inside champion and developed an insider's reputation. This same scenario is easily adaptable to various geographic regions and marketplace sectors.

An Insider's Reputation Will Help Keep Rivals Out

Another client of ours established a unique niche clientele. He's a financial advisor and he targets airline pilots. He has done this so well he can saunter up to a group of unknown airline pilots in an airport and intelligently participate in their conversation and can even use the lingo which comes only from associating with pilots on a very regular basis. This gift of the aeronautical gab is not accidental.

This advisor started his narrowcasting efforts with two of his clients that were pilots. It was accidental that he attracted the two in the first place, they didn't know each other. But once he realized that he had an untapped opportunity in the form of these potential inside champions, he invited both of them out to lunch and began the process of developing an insiders reputation. "I'm fascinated with what you do. I really like working with airline pilots. They are terrific people. In a perfect world, I would like to deal extensively with people just like you. Would you please help me understand how to become more attractive to people in your line of work?"

He then asked his pilot clients the following questions:
- Please tell me more about what the life of a pilot is like.
- What challenges do you face?
- What is important to you?
- What could make your life better?
- What publications could I read to better understand your industry?

This advisor now deals with many airline pilots. His reputation precedes him. He is now the *"go-to guy"* for pilots. Anytime the subject of money comes up with one of his pilot-clients and their inner circle, it is a knee-jerk reaction for his clients to say, "You have to go see my advisor. He understands us."

The Law of Environment tells us people tend to congregate with other people who are pretty much like themselves. Doctors associate with other doctors, chiropractors with chiropractors, and so forth. If you decide to become a specialist for a particular sector, use the Law of Environment to your advantage. One of your clients will be at a gathering with others in your chosen demographic, someone will probably raise the subject of business providers, your area of expertise, and express dissatisfaction with their current situation. Armed with the dedicated Advocate Process you have put in place, your client will make a compelling case for you.

Although some generalist business owners have done very well trying to be all things to all people, those who have built their business by offering focused services to a particular sector have a distinct and simple advantage. Their clients have a great story to tell. It's compelling to hear about someone who specializes in dealing with people who are just like you. Why would you want to go anywhere else? Best of all, the disciplines of specializing compound. In time, your effort takes on a life of its own and then the dominos start to fall.

So You've Decided to Specialize . . . . Now What?

It is crucial that you understand what is referred to in marketing as "the stage-of-readiness." When you identify your specific target markets, resign yourself to the fact that you don't know when the prospects you're targeting will be ready to talk to you. It's just a matter of time but it will take time. Again, from personal experience, we know that in your attempts to build contrast and predisposition, you have to build a degree of familiarity and comfort with a prospective client. Understanding this will remind you to be patient and save you some stress. Remember, stress in business stems from a lot of things, including unrealistic expectations. The gap between when you want something to happen and when it actually happens is often where stress is borne.

Your prospecting efforts are designed to also counter the Law of Diminishing Intent. This immutable law simply reminds us that when people consider taking action on something they had better act immediately. If they don't, their intent will diminish and fade. This occurs in marketing. A prospective client considers a prospecting offer. If they put it off, the likelihood they will act later diminishes. Keep in mind, they aren't necessarily saying "no." They could be saying "not now" or "I don't know", which is why you need to implement a campaign that follows the fundamentals below.

The first concept is called **AICA**, an acronym (naturally) that frames the concept of prospecting with these four tenets: Attention, Interest, Confidence and Action.

Attention. Obviously, prospects get bombarded with countless marketing messages. Yours has to stand out and get their attention. Whether it's a flyer, an ad in the yellow pages, email marketing, a search engine campaign or a direct mail letter, you need a hook to get the person's attention immediately. The headline at the top of your advertising vehicle must say something that speaks to the prospect and shakes him or her out of their fog. If you study marketing, you will find that most headlines make a promise statement of something positive or present a problem the prospect can relate to. More on that in a second.

For purposes of illustration, we'll use direct mail as our marketing medium example. For what it's worth, we are big fans of extremely well targeted "small-batch" direct mail campaigns. Many people would, in this era, dismiss direct mail as being obsolete. The concept is not flawed, 9 out of 10 campaigns themselves are flawed.

People still like getting mail but most of us sort it over a garbage can. If the mail you send is not distinctive and doesn't get the recipients attention, you might as well throw it in your own garbage can and save the stamps.

Believe it or not, a great way to get a recipients instant attention is to use lumpy mail. A small-batch campaign with something lumpy like a fridge magnet will always outperform a larger campaign sent to more people but without the lumpy insert.

So, let's assume they open your letter, you then need to encourage them to read it. As mentioned, the opening headline must get their attention. We just hinted at this but allow us to expand on the headline concept by integrating yet another acronym, **PAS**, within AICA. PAS stands for **Problem, Agitate, Solve**. The best headline you can use in any letter or any campaign of any kind is to present a problem that the reader can relate with. Every time someone actually reads your marketing piece, they either connect with it and say "me too" or they dismiss it and say "so what". A problem is a perfect way to achieve the "me too" connection.

For example, a landscape architect sending a campaign to an affluent neighborhood could use the following headline:

"The Top 10 Mistakes Homeowners Make When Landscaping"

An accountant targeting business owners could use this headline: **"The 7 Most Common Tax Planning Mistakes and How to Avoid Them"**

You get the idea. The headline must be clear and specific and it must get their attention. It doesn't always have to be a negative connotation either. For example, when someone is considering our coaching and consulting services, we submit an article we wrote called **"The Top 10 Questions to Ask Before Hiring a Coach."** That headline is a "me too" primarily because if someone is considering hiring a coach they want to make an informed decision.

Stand Out From the Pack with AICA

O nce you have the reader's attention, you then want to hold their attention and **build their interest.** Consider what legendary marketing guru David Ogilvie said, "You can't bore someone into buying something." Most marketing efforts are long winded data-dumps that aren't compelling. There is a marketing precept that states, "Facts tell, stories sell." The best way to shift a campaign from a "so what" to a "me too" is tell a story that the reader can connect with or paint a picture with a specific episode that the reader can relate with. Using our Top 10 Questions to Ask Before Hiring a Coach article as a further example, the opening paragraphs create a scene of a person who has decided they want to hire a coach but is uncertain about how to choose. You can see the article in the Actionable CD-ROM to understand the concept of building interest with this approach.

The C in AICA stands for confidence. Once you have their attention and their interest builds, you have to strengthen their confidence to buy. The best way to do this is to use what is called social-proof. People want to know what other people like them are saying as a result of taking action. Well placed testimonials are perfect evidence. On our website, for example, there is a button that says *"Click to read and hear what clients are saying."* What your clients say about you is far more persuasive than anything you can say about yourself.

To prove our point on both targeting and social-proof, we know of a guy who owns a window washing firm that caters to wealthy homeowners. He started by selecting affluent neighborhoods and then offered to do a few homes with an introductory cut-rate offer. On the day that he was booked to perform the service, he would knock on the doors of the neighbors pretending to be lost. The neighbor would answer the door and the window washer would greet him or her and say, "I'm here to clean the Henderson's windows, do you know which house is theirs?" We're not kidding. And of course this led to others in the neighborhood signing up for his service. After all, if he was good enough for the Henderson's....

The last *A* in AICA stands for *action*. Always ask them to take action. But make it easy to opt in. Take the abstract of what you do down to something non-threatening, easy to conceptualize, non-committal and differentiate it with value. Every single marketing effort should encourage a learning experience. Provide something value-added that people will actually find to be of value. Again, in our article, <u>The Top 10 Questions to Ask Before Hiring a Coach</u>, we say right up front "Whether or not you hire us is secondary at this point. Use this document as part of your due diligence process before you hire any coach or consultant and ask them these questions." And the article provides the list of questions. How valuable is that? It requires no commitment and the questions are absolutely essential for everyone to ask before hiring a coach.

Give Them Something Meaningful to Ask For

Whatever your profession is, you can create a *Top 10 Questions to Ask* document and make it the call-to-action that you invite your prospective clients to ask for it.

Contrast that to what most people use. For example, you see a bus bench ad for a real estate agent. It looks like every other billboard ad for a real estate agent you've ever seen and probably has the same bland call-to-action every other agent uses, "Call for a free home evaluation." So what! (He'd be better off standing outside tearing up $20 bills on a windy day – he'd get the attention of more passing motorists with that technique than with the easy-to-dismiss ad.)

What if the call-to-action read "Call us to receive this report: <u>The Top 10 Questions to Ask Before Buying a House in (your neighborhood)</u>"?

The beautiful thing about the AICA and PAS methodology is that it can be applied to virtually all marketing efforts. So use it as a frame of reference in the future.

DRIP On Them

O k, so you've identified your target market and you've created your campaign. Now what? You need to launch the campaign. You may be shocked to read this but we have (yet another) acronym for you. And this one is **DRIP** which stands for **Discipline, Respect, Inform** and **Persist**.

In all of your marketing efforts **it is essential that you be *disciplined*.** Be disciplined in your targeting. Be disciplined in your distribution. Don't get faked out into thinking, "More is more. I'll send out more." We all get junk mail all the time from companies offering furnace cleaning, lawn care, etc. Most of it is easy to dismiss and forget because most of it is sent "one-off". This means we receive it once and then probably never again. By using frequency in your distribution, you create familiarity and that positions you for when the recipient's stage-of-readiness kicks in. We would much rather you send a string of seven 500 direct mail pieces linked and sequentially tied to each other over a seven month period than to send 3500 pieces one-off. Each DRIP triggers a moment of recognition that builds confidence and trust. When you build AICA and PAS into each DRIP, you are putting the odds in your favor that eventually the prospective client will warm up to you.

The *R* in DRIP is for respect. Lean with respect. Much of the DRIP marketing used today is annoying, which explains why we are not the biggest fans of cold-calling – it's not respectful. Think about all the cold calls you get. The ultimate disrespectful interruption. Do you really want to be in the same category? Be practical, be strategic and ask yourself, "How does this reflect on us?" Consider too, if a new client is going to be swayed by a cold call, how much can you expect in terms of loyalty from this person?

If you do want to reach out with a phone call, why not send a string of 3 linked and sequential direct mail pieces and then follow-up with a phone call? This way you can point to the information in the three pieces and make your call-to-action a reinforcement to your offer. The best way to be respectful is to bring as much value as possible. And one the best ways to bring real value is in the **I** in DRIP. **Inform. Be Informative.**

Teach Prospects Something

Teach people something they probably don't know about your sector. Offer meaningful information that they can translate into results. Our **Top 10 Lists** for example bring value that readers can use regardless of whether or not they do business with us. That is *informative*. Also, look at how the word FORM exists within the word informative. Value-added content can include relevant information that goes beyond your message. If you are targeting business owners for example, your value-added content can speak to their occupation as well as your message. Many good accountants provide value-added financial tips that their clients can relay to their kids – family. FORM can be a tremendous point of difference to help your prospecting efforts stand out from the pack.

Another way to make your efforts informative is to simply make the information you send easy to read and process. With letters, or any form of advertising, ensure it has a **Dual Readership Path**. What does this mean? For example, you're at the airport and you're about to take a trip so you want to buy a magazine. You grab Esquire or Vanity Fair or whatever catches your eye. You don't necessarily buy it right off the bat, you stand there for a few minutes. You look at the cover to see if anything interests you and you flip through it to see if anything gets your attention. You see an article. Do you start reading it word for word? No. You do a panoramic scan of the article looking at pictures, statements in bold font and at the pull quotes.

What are pull quotes? They're bold quotes sprinkled throughout the article to engage your interest. You're interested so you fold it up and pay for it. (You may have noticed that there are bolded comments, quotes and other features designed to break up the content of this book. This enables someone who is casually perusing it a chance to get a sense for the ideas and theme quickly.)

Use the same approach in all forms of your promotional efforts. Remember AICA. If we send you a letter, it'll have the introductory components, then it'll have a bold hook. We'll present a problem to which you can relate. And then it'll have text. Between the first and second paragraph will be another bold statement, maybe to agitate the problem, and then another bit of text and then one more bold statement which makes a promise about our solution. Problem, agitate, solve and then the call-to-action in the text. Here's the point. When you open the letter, do you start reading it word for word? No. You scan it. You'll look at the bold text and probably the PS at the bottom. You may find it interesting to know this approach speaks to both the left and right brain. Right brain people don't look for as much detail as left brain. The body of the text gives you detail. The words in bold get your attention. Use this in your emails, in your ads, whatever the case may be.

The *P* in DROP stands for Persist. If you are narrowcasting and specializing in your prospecting efforts, be persistent. There's an old saying, "If you're well-targeted, drip on them 'til they buy or die." It may take 7 letters, it may take 17 hits before they actually opt-in and engage. If it's well-targeted, what you're trying to do through "frequency and recent-cy" is contrast yourself to their current provider, distance yourself from everybody else and build a relationship of value because you're fast-tracking them to advocacy. We don't mean to oversimplify prospecting by just glancing off some of these points. We want to give you some fundamentals. Are you targeted? Is there value? Are you being persistent?

When all of these prospecting concepts pay off and you start meeting with the people you attract, be certain to employ the consultative approach we discussed earlier in the book. Use an agenda, have no hidden agenda and strive for fit based on your AAA ideal client profile.

Most salespeople look at the sales process as being linear with the end point being the sale. The salesperson creates an emotional state in order to motivate a customer to satisfy a real or perceived need. Motivation is mistaken for trust in this process. 80% of all effort is spent completing the process and making the 'close', the 'sale', or 'doing the deal'. The customer is then left with a product which satisfied the emotional state used to power the sale. At the end of this process the salesperson must look for a new sale to make, using the remaining 20% of his effort to get back in front of past customers. The treadmill continues from sale to sale.

Consultation is a dynamic cycle based on gaining permission to proceed with a proposed course of action. In order to be granted permission, the consultant seeks to understand a need and then brings professional insight to planning and arranging a solution. Unlike the sales process, the consultation process invests 80% of effort into enhancing the relationship by validating and strengthening the mutually agreed upon partnership between client and consultant. Only 20% of effort is expended on agreeing to results. The consultant does not need to continually feed the emotional state of the client. In other words, consultants continue to increase the value of the relationship by demonstrating solutions rather than the need to purchase a product. The result is that the client becomes an advocate instead of remaining a client or customer. An advocate will bring more of their personal business to the consultant and will encourage others to seek the trusted services the consultant provides.

We've talked about strategic analysis, we've talked about targets and goals, we've talked about actions based on cause and effect - the activities in which you must engage. We're hoping you go back to your existing clients and their prospective promotional partners, based on CAST (the client advisory support team concept) and stimulate enough new business in those areas to the point where prospecting is a bonus. For most entrepreneurs, prospecting is their engine. They spend so much time on new clients they almost punish existing clients because they're going after new business at the expense of the people already on board. Don't focus on gathering all these new relationships. We'd much rather see your business thrive with 300 advocates than watch you work long hours for 1,000 customers and clients.

Remember

All of your prospect target marketing efforts must:

- Get their ATTENTION – *Is it a "me too" or a "so what"?*
- Hold their INTEREST – *Facts tell, stories sell*
- Build their CONFIDENCE – *Use social-proof*
- Ask for their ACTION – *Give them something to ask for*

-and-

- Present a PROBLEM they can relate to
- Expand and AGITATE the problem
- Offer a solid SOLUTON to the problem

-and-

- Be DISCIPLINED
- Be RESPECTFUL
- Be INFORMATIVE
- Be PERSISTENT

Take Action Now! (Week 12)

- Review the Target Marketing Checklist on the Actionable CD-ROM and use it to scrutinize your current prospecting efforts.

Section 4: Reality Check

Holding Yourself Accountable

"If it is to be, it is up to me."

When put together, those are ten of the most powerful words ever written.

Once you've conducted your Strategic Analysis, established your Targets and Goals and created an Action Plan, all you need to do to finish the STAR process is to do a personal **Reality Check**.

If you've gotten this far in our process, you are obviously serious about taking your business to the next level. The first question you have to ask yourself at this point is this, "What kind of person do I need to become to bring my plan to reality?"

We are constantly asking ourselves that question. We never get tired of it because we are constantly evolving and challenging ourselves to achieve new heights.

Because of our fixation on execution, the beauty of holding yourself accountable is that it reminds you, "after all is said and done, more is often said than done."

Don't Let Your Intent Diminish

We've seen how procrastination and the Law of Diminishing Intent can rob an entrepreneur of the quantifiable results that can come from implementing relevant strategies and concepts.

If we want things to change in our business, we have to change. It starts with the leadership. We absolutely must be committed to self-development and refinement in order to attract the kind of clients and have the kind of business we want. A mentor once told us, "Income rarely exceeds self-development." Formal education can get us a job, make us a living. With self-education, how high is high? To earn more, we really must learn more. So be a serious student because everything you want to get better at is a study.

Secrets to Success?

Secondly, there are no secrets. We all see books, CDs and websites talking about the secrets of success. They're not secrets. It's not new. It might be new to you, it might be new to me, but there are no secrets. It is all about skills. And the great thing about it is that the books are already written waiting for us to read them. Everything is a study. Marketing is a study. Practice management is a study. Business development is a study. Parenting is a study. Marriage is a study. Be a serious student. To earn more, we must learn more. To achieve more, we must learn more. To attract more attractive clients, we have to make ourselves more attractive. And that is achieved by being a serious student.

We'll say it again, the value of this book begins right now. What are you going to implement? We haven't said anything you haven't heard 100 times. We've provided gentle reminders. But perhaps now you are ready for implementation. As Confucius said, "When the student is ready, the teacher will appear."

Build your business plan, using the worksheets, fill in all the blanks to create yourself a great roadmap. Start right now. You could email your plan to your top ten competitors without a worry in the world. Why? Because they're locked in the status quo. And you're not.

What are you prepared to do differently? Think about it.

What are you prepared to do right now, before the Law of Diminishing Intent kicks in? Will you use an agenda in all your meetings? Will you start doing the call rotations? How about the service matrix?

If you could do only one thing, what would it be? One thing. If the one thing you did was sit down with your people and explain the Loyalty Ladder and the concept of advocacy and buying into something instead of buying something, this would be a good use of your time. If you called your 50 AAA clients and your team called the 200 other clients as part of the call rotation, that alone would make a difference. If the one thing you did was use an agenda in your meetings with everybody, this would be a good use of your time.

What does it take to move forward with a new plan, to make sure nothing stands in the way of our success? Very simply, it is imperative we take action right away. It doesn't matter what we do to forge ahead. It only matters that we make sure we do something to get the ball rolling. The sooner we put our plans into action, the more likely we are to achieve our goals.

All Systems Go!

One of the most important changes you can make is to adopt a systems-based approach to your business. Every process and activity you and your team execute on a daily basis is planned, scripted, rehearsed, refined and well-documented in a procedure manual. Before you dismiss this as trivial and tedious, consider two key reasons why you should script your business from top to bottom.

1. Until your methodology is documented, it is not an intellectual property or asset.
2. If you don't document everything, chances are your business won't run smoothly unless you are there.

Systems ensure you aren't at the mercy of talent alone when it comes to your support staff. Our lawyer's business is held together by his legal assistant. He recently said, "Every time she returns from holiday, I have to give her a raise because she can see how the business nearly caved in without her."

Don't rely on maverick talent. Develop talent by creating a systematic approach you can hand to someone else to implement. You are truly on the verge of greatness when you have made yourself obsolete. Strive for the day when your business can run like a Swiss watch without you being there all the time. It's not only liberating, it's rejuvenating.

The primary benefits of a systems-based operating approach are improved predictability and efficiency. Think of your business and marketing plans as road maps. Your operating manual serves as your Global Positioning Satellite device. Without this approach, it would be like walking though uncharted territory at night with only a flash-light. A good plan, driven by systems, would be like a beacon guiding you. It lets you see past short-term obstacles without the risk of drifting off course.

You've given a lot to your business. It's time to get something back. Increased efficiency leads to more free time and you'll be able to re-charge your batteries and balance your life.

This journey won't be without trials and frustrations. Shifting to an operational approach requires patience while it gains traction. It will require constant tinkering while you find the right mix of processes. But it will be necessary if you want to take your business to the next level and if you want to avoid obsolescence.

Think of exercise. If you did 40 push-ups right now, the last five or ten would contribute most to building strength. However, the first 30 were necessary before you could get to the last 10 and derive a benefit. You've already done the first 30 in your business by honing your sales and marketing skills and refining your industry-specific knowledge. Finish the job and take your business to the next level by making the adjustments to your business that are certain to add quantifiable impact. Your confidence and interest in your business, not to mention your sense of fulfillment, will be stronger than ever.

Thank you for taking time to read and consider our advice and opinions. It means a lot to us. Contact us with any questions you may have. Until then, best of success with your business.

Remember
• Drive yourself and in the process you will drive systems, drive sales and drive results.

Take Action Now! (Week 12)
• Review the Accountability Worksheets in the Actionable CD-ROM to begin the process of translating these ideas into measurable results.

CD-ROM Actionable Templates

Week 1:
- STAR Business Planning Tool (ongoing)
- Sample Organizational and Structural Chart

Week 2 & 3:
- Sample Procedure Manual Menu
- AAA Ideal Client Profile Tool

Week 4:
- Sample FORM Client Profiling Tool
- Goal Setting Worksheets

Week 5:
- Sample Service Matrix
- Sample Call Rotation Scripting

Week 6:
- Sample Client Advisory Council Campaign
- Sample Agendas

Week 7:
- Sample Customer Conversion Tool

Week 8:

- Sample Advocate Process

Week 9:

- Sample Referral Scripting

Week 10:

- CAST Strategic Alliance Scripting

Week 11:

- Client Milestone and Moment-of-Truth Guidelines

Week 12:

- Target Marketing Checklist
- Sample Action Planning Accountability Worksheets

About Pareto Systems' Customized Coaching and Consulting Services

Have You Hit a Plateau With Your Business?

Pareto Systems and 8020Platform co-founders Duncan MacPherson and David Miller lead a team of dedicated business development and practice management consultants who help individual entrepreneurs translate ideas and concepts into results.

Their time-tested curriculum of actionable solutions can be sequentially deployed in a turnkey fashion. You will be able identify and capitalize on untapped opportunities that exist within your business and create a blueprint of proven strategies. Your personal coach will hold you and your team accountable as you embark on the step-by-step implementation process, which includes:

- How to Competitor-Proof Your Clients Using a Service Matrix
- How to Create Consistency and Build Trusting Client Relationships
- How to Fully Capitalize on The Pareto Principal (80/20 Rule)
- How to Attract a Higher Quality and Quantity of Referrals
- How to Deploy Predictable and Sustainable Systems

Our Diagnostic Assessment Process helps you and us determine if we are a good fit for you. Contact us at 866.593.8020 to set up an introductory phone meeting.

Visit www.paretosystems.com to read *The Top Ten Questions to Ask Before Hiring a Coach* article. While you are there you can also learn more about our:

- Speaking Engagements
- Corporate Consulting Solutions
- Content Licensing and Private Label Services
- Management Train-the-Trainer Programs
- Bulk orders of this book for your favorite clients. (Call 800-215-3294)

Take Your Business to the Next Level - Starting Right Now!

Pareto Systems and 8020Platform co-founders Duncan MacPherson and David Miller have created a web-based business development and practice management dashboard that can propel your business to new heights quickly and efficiently.

This on-demand solution is available on a monthly subscription basis and is accessible 24/7 and is designed to enable you and your team to methodically implement our actionable concepts.

8020Platform - Proven Strategies

Our entry level internet based system gives you and your team 24/7 access to our time-tested business building strategies with on-going updates. Your personalized dashboard also provides you with a:

- Customizable Organizational and Structural Chart
- Personalized Procedures Manual
- Service Matrix
- Advocate Service Processes

Contact us at 866-593-8020 for a one month free trial.

8020Platform - Client Relationship Manager (CRM)

Our flagship solution gives you all of the great practice management and business development functionality found in the proven strategies version AND is fully integrated on a robust Client Relationship Management platform. This one-of-a-kind turnkey solution is all you and your team need to manage client relationships and run your business with precision and predictability. In addition, you will receive:

- AAA Client Relationship Journals
- FORM Client Chemistry System
- Full Array of Automated Processes
- Milestone Recognition and DART Deployment
- Remote Access and Team Oversight Features

Visit www.8020platform.com for pricing, demo information and special trial offers.

Contact us at 866-593-8020 for a one month free trial.

Notes

Notes

_____

_____

_____

_____

_____

_____

_____

_____

_____

_____

_____

_____

_____

_____

_____

_____

_____

_____